Introduction

Lying between the Vale of Clwyd and the Sno
wild, beautiful, unspoilt and largely unexplor
generally by-passed by walkers and tourists alike
Snowdonia. At its heart is Mynydd Hiraethog – often referred to as the
'Denbigh Moors', a large undulating upland plateau containing an expansive
tract of heather moorland – a Site of Special Scientific Interest. The area has
been occupied by man since about 5700 B.C. when a better climate and
woodland habitat first attracted nomadic hunters, and contains important
Bronze Age ceremonial and burial sites and Iron-Age hillforts. From the
Middle Ages to the 19th century black cattle, often from Anglesey, were
grazed on the upland pastures before being taken to market in England.

More recently the character of Hiraethog has changed with the creation of
Clocaenog Forest – a habitat for red squirrels – and the construction of several large reservoirs, including Llyn Brenig with its recreational amenities.

Much of Hiraethog and its adjoining low hills remains to be discovered.
Easily accessible, it offers excellent walking with a great sense of space and
superb views, especially of the mountains of Snowdonia. Recently, a
Denbighshire/Conwy Council/community initiative has developed the footpath network and established a waymarked linear Mynydd Hiraethog trail
linking the area's scattered villages. I hope that my routes, some of which
were researched during the wettest Autumn on record, will help to open up
more of this beautiful landscape.

The twenty-one circular walks in this book explore its moorland, open
hills, river valleys, lakes, old drovers' roads, ancient communities, woods
and forests, whilst providing an insight into the area's history.

The routes, which range from a 2¼ mile lakeside ramble to a 10½ mile
moorland 'yomp', follow public rights of way or permissive paths. *A key fea-
ture is that most individual routes, as well as containing shorter walk
options, can easily be linked to provide longer and more challenging day
walks, if required.* Be suitably equipped, especially on the more remote
exposed moorland routes, which can be boggy. Walking boots are recom-
mended, along with appropriate clothing to protect against the elements.
Please remember that the condition of paths can vary according to season
and weather. Please refer any problems encountered with paths to the rele-
vant Highways Department (Denbighshire or Conwy Councils). Each walk
has a detailed map and description which enables the route to be followed
without difficulty, but be aware that changes in detail can occur at any time.
The location of each walk is shown on the back cover and a summary of their
key features is also given. This includes an estimated walking time, but allow
more time to enjoy the scenery. Please observe the country code.

Enjoy your walking!

WALK 1
AFON CLYWEDOG & FOEL GANOL

DESCRIPTION A delightful 4-mile walk exploring the valleys and hills near Cyffylliog – an old community set in the wooded Clywedog valley some 4 miles west of Ruthin – offering extensive views. The route, which is part of a waymarked Mynydd Hiraethog circuit, follows a lovely section of the Clywedog river, then rises up an attractive side valley to follow a high-level country road along the northern slopes of Foel Ganol. It then descends on a delightful open green track, and road back to Cyffylliog. An equally enjoyable alternative descent route is included. Allow about 2½ hours. The Red Lion, a traditional village inn offering good food and drink, makes a good finish to the walk.

START Cyffylliog [SJ 060578]

DIRECTIONS From Ruthin take the B5105 towards Cerrigydrudion and just after passing Llanfwrog church, take the road signposted to Cyffylliog. Go through Bontuchel and cross the river into Cyffylliog, where there is limited roadside parking.

According to folklore, the parish was haunted by mischievous fairies, who used to take horses from their stables and ride them all night, returning them dirty and exhausted. So, it is best to explore this area during daylight hours – just in case!

1 From the centre of the village, take the road signposted to Nantglyn. Soon you pass the old Georgian 'hearse house' and medieval Church of St. Mary founded in the 15th C. 100 yards beyond the church, turn RIGHT on a waymarked path passing the end of a house to cross a footbridge over the Afon Clywedog. Follow the path LEFT, passing beneath the house of Tunnel Road and across its access track to go through a small gate. Now follow a delightful scenic path alongside the river. When it splits, keep straight ahead to cross a stile by a gate. Continue along the field edge, through a gate, across a stream, and on down a green track beneath a cottage. After going through a gate, go half-RIGHT to follow another wide track through a forest. The track runs for a while above the fast-flowing river, then rises gently to a waymark post, before dropping down to another waymark post at a track junction. Turn RIGHT up the track and follow it through the forest to cross a stile by a gate – *with good views across the Concwest valley.*

2 Here you leave the waymarked circuit by continuing straight ahead on a green track, which climbs steadily up the western slopes of Foel Uchaf to reach a road. Turn RIGHT and follow this attractive quiet upland country road as it contours along the northern slopes of Foel Ganol – *providing steady walking and extensive open views: north towards Denbigh, the northern Clwydians, and the coast at Rhyl; and ahead to the central Clwydian Hills, extending south from Moel y Parc with its T.V. transmitter mast to the highest point-Moel Famau, with its distinctive ruined Jubilees Tower – and on to Moel Fenlli, with its iron-age fort. After ¾ mile, when the road splits by an old farm, swing RIGHT with the road.*

3 Here you have a choice of return routes. For the main route (**A**) continue along the road, and at a cattle-grid, go half-LEFT on the waymarked path to follow a delightful green track across the open upland pasture of Moel y Fron – *with extensive views west.* As the track begins to descend, passing the tiny Llyn Gloyw, new views unfold of the Clwydian hills and the Llantisilio Mountains. Eventually the track ends at a road. Turn RIGHT and follow the road down into Cyffylliog.

*(For the alternative route (**B**), about 100 yards beyond the farm, cross a stile on the right by a waymark post, and follow a green track along the field edge parallel with the road. Soon the track swings down to pass the cottage of Foel Ganol. At its garden corner, go through a gate and on down a large field to go through a gateway in the corner. Continue down the next field, parallel with the tree boundary on your right, and just beyond its end, swing half-LEFT to cross a*

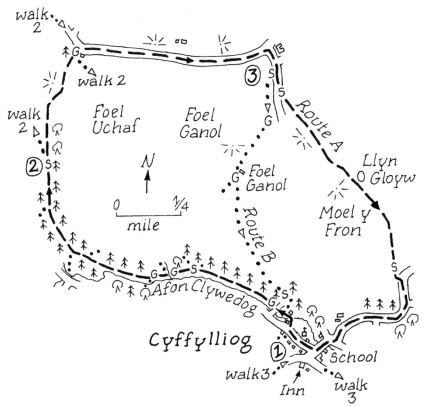

walk 2

walk 2

walk 2

walk 2

Foel Uchaf

Foel Ganol

(3)

Route A

Llyn O Gloyw

Foel Ganol

Moel y Fron

N

0   ¼
mile

Route B

Afon Clywedog

Cyffylliog

(1)

School

walk 3

Inn

walk 3

stile into a wood. Go ahead to drop down through the trees, soon swinging RIGHT behind Tunnel Road, then turning LEFT with

the path to drop steeply down through its gardens to join your outward route.)

Hearse House

WALK 2

CLYWEDOG RESERVOIR & FOEL UCHAF

DESCRIPTION A 9 mile stretched figure of eight walk featuring attractive wooded river valleys, open hills, forest, a scenic upland reservoir and excellent views. The route also offers an alternative 3¾ (**B**) or 4½ (**C**) mile walk around Foel Uchaf. The main walk (**A**) follows part of a waymarked Mynydd Hiraethog path along the attractive Clywedog and Concwest valleys, before rising steadily on lanes and open/forestry tracks to reach the Clywedog reservoir, lying at over 1300 feet amongst forest and moorland. The return route crosses upland pasture, returns to the Concwest valley, then follows an attractive upland road, before crossing Foel Uchaf and making a delightful descent back into the Clywedog valley. Allow about 4½ hours.
START Cyffylliog [SJ 060578] See **Walk 1**.

1 Follow instructions for the first section of Walk 1.

2 (For **Walk B** continue ahead up the green track. Just before it reaches the road at point 5, turn right along another track and continue with the main described route). For **Walks A** and **C**, go half-LEFT with the waymarked Mynydd Hiraethog path to cross another stile. Continue in the same direction along the top field edge, soon through an area of gorse, to reach a waymark post. Here, go half-LEFT through an area of reed and thistle, to cross a stile in a fence corner. Continue ahead alongside a fence and on to follow a path by or near the Afon Concwest, along the bottom edge of a delightful area of predominantly oak woodland. After crossing a stile, keep on by the river, over another stile, and on to reach a road. (For **Walk C**, turn right and follow the road to point **5**.)

3 Turn LEFT and follow the road up to a junction. Turn RIGHT up a lane (no through road). After a while the lane levels out to pass Bryn-ochan. After passing a ruin on your right, swing LEFT with the lane to its end at a large house and cattle-grid. Continue ahead with a track – *enjoying panoramic views across the Clywedog valley to the Clwydian Hills*. The track then gently descends alongside a forest to a track junction. Continue up the RIGHT fork. After going through a gate, follow the stony track as it rises steadily through the forest. *As you get higher, forest clearance provides good views of the deep gorge at the narrow head of the valley.* After just over a mile you reach the unexpected sight of Clywedog reservoir. *This lovely stretch of water, popular with wildfowl and fishermen, makes a pleasant place for a stop.*

4 Return along the track, and when it bends right, turn LEFT up another forestry track. After about 150 yards, go half-RIGHT on a bridleway through the forest. Leave it by a gate and follow the boundary on your right, at first alongside the forest, to cross a stile in the fence corner. *Pause to enjoy the stunning views: ahead the Clwydian Hills stretching south from Moel y parc with its T.V. transmitter mast, over several hillforts, and Moel Famau, towards the Horseshoe Pass and the Llantisilio Mountains; to the south are the distant Berwyns.* Now go half-LEFT across upland pasture grazed by sheep, dropping down towards the house that you passed earlier. Cross a stile in the field corner and go through two gates to rejoin the lane. Follow it back to the road junction. Turn LEFT down the road back to point **3**. Follow the road up to a junction. Turn RIGHT, past a side road, and follow the steadily rising road. *This attractive quiet upland country road running between hedgerows of hawthorn, hazel, blackthorn, bramble, raspberry, honeysuck-*

Clywedog Reservoir

4

le, rowan, elderberry, gorse, wild rose, and a variety of flowers, is a delight to walk along.

5 After passing another side road, go through a gate on your right by a way-mark post and a corrugated shed. Follow a track up across the northern slopes of Foel Uchaf. At a prominent viewpoint – *with superb views looking north to Denbigh and down the Vale of Clwyd to the coast* – the track swings RIGHT south across Foel Uchaf – *soon offering good views of the Clywedog valley and the southern Clwydian Hills.* Follow the track down, and just after it swings LEFT towards a farm, cross a stile on the right by a waymark post. Walk down a green track to cross a fence corner. Go ahead a few yards, then swing sharp LEFT to follow a track along the edge of a forest, soon swinging RIGHT through the trees. When the track splits, take the LEFT fork to cross a gate at the forest edge. Go down the field towards a cottage, soon alongside a stream on your left. Pass through a small wooden gate to the left of the cottage, and go on down its access track. When it bends right, turn LEFT and simply follow your outward route back to the start.

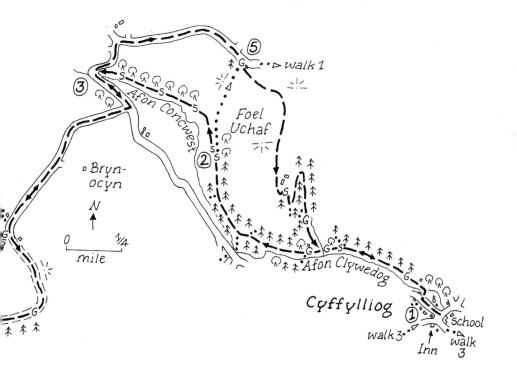

WALK 3
PINCYN LLYS FROM CYFFYLLIOG

DESCRIPTION A 7-mile walk through undulating upland pasture and forest to the top of Pincyn Llys, with its unusual stone monument and panoramic views. Allow about 3½ hours. A shorter 3¼ mile walk is included.
START Cyffylliog [SJ 060578] See **Walk 1**.

Pincyn Llys is a part-forested hill (1354 feet) lying between Cyffylliog and Clocaenog. The monument was erected in 1830 by the Second Lord Bagot to commemorate the planting of forest. A later inscription records that the plantation was felled during and after the 1914-18 war, and Clocaenog Forest was created in 1930. The monument stands at the corner of an ancient earthwork known as 'Llys y Frenhines' - 'The Queen's Court House' - from which a boulder shaped like an armchair called 'Cader y Frenhines' ('The Queen's Chair') was removed to Lord Bagot's residence at Pool Park in 1804.

1 Take the minor road leading east from the Red Lion, past a phone box. Follow it for about 1¼ miles. About 200 yards beyond Tyddyn-Bach, swing RIGHT off the road to cross a stile by a gate. Follow a rising green track, soon swinging LEFT along a wood edge. Shortly swing RIGHT with the track. It becomes more of a path and rises gently through the trees. It soon swings RIGHT again, and after about 20 yards, go half-LEFT on a path up through the trees to leave the forest by a stile. Continue ahead up the large field, passing a solitary tree and on to cross a stile in a fence corner. Continue along the field edge, go through a gate and follow the boundary round to cross a ladder-stile. Continue with the field edge, over another stile, then go across the next field and through a gate ahead. Now go half-RIGHT down to cross a gate in the field corner. Turn LEFT along a stony track (*or right for the* **shorter** *walk: follow the track/lane down*).

2 After going through a gate, swing LEFT up with the track, over a stile by a barn and on past the old farm. Follow a green track to cross a stile by a gate, and on up to cross another stile. Continue up the delightful green track and on through a clearing in the forest. At a road, follow it RIGHT, then shortly turn LEFT on a path signposted to Pincyn Llys. Continue through open forest, over a cross path. After crossing a track, the path rises to reach the Bagot monument on Pincyn Llys. From the monument take a path heading south, soon dropping steeply down through the trees, over a forestry track, and on down to a forestry road.

3 Turn RIGHT and follow the main forestry road for nearly ½ mile to reach a road. Turn LEFT and follow the road for about ¾ mile to a junction. Turn RIGHT, and at the next junction by a house, continue ahead on a waymarked path along a lane. Follow it along the forest edge and soon after passing a farm entrance, turn RIGHT by a waymark post to follow a green track. Continue ahead across open pasture. After crossing a stile drop down the field ahead to go through a gate by a ruin. Continue along an enclosed green track. At Cae Gwyn, swing LEFT down its access lane and then continue down a road into Cyffylliog.

WALK 4
PINCYN LLYS FROM CLOCAENOG

DESCRIPTION A 6 mile walk along open side valleys and through forest to Pincyn Llys. Allow about 3 hours.
START Clocaenog [SJ 084542]
DIRECTIONS Clocaenog is signposted from the B5105 Cerrigydrudion – Ruthin road. Park tidily near the junction opposite the school.

1 Take the road opposite the school and follow it past houses. When it bends right by the former National School – *built by Lord*

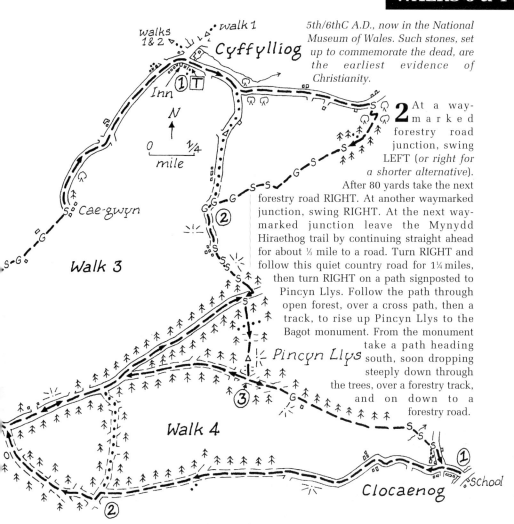

5th/6thC A.D., now in the National Museum of Wales. Such stones, set up to commemorate the dead, are the earliest evidence of Christianity.

2 At a way-marked forestry road junction, swing LEFT (or right for a shorter alternative). After 80 yards take the next forestry road RIGHT. At another waymarked junction, swing RIGHT. At the next way-marked junction leave the Mynydd Hiraethog trail by continuing straight ahead for about ⅓ mile to a road. Turn RIGHT and follow this quiet country road for 1¼ miles, then turn RIGHT on a path signposted to Pincyn Llys. Follow the path through open forest, over a cross path, then a track, to rise up Pincyn Llys to the Bagot monument. From the monument take a path heading south, soon dropping steeply down through the trees, over a forestry track, and on down to a forestry road.

Bagot and once catering for 60 children daily and 45 on Sundays – go up a lane to St. Foddyd's church. *Dating from 1538 and restored in the 19thC, it contains many interesting features, including a fine 16thC rood screen, a 15thC font, and a bell, dating from 1638, which is still rung before each service.* Continue along the leafy lane, passing a large old farm. After about ¾ mile, when the lane swings left to a cattle grid, continue up the track ahead. When the track meets a forestry road continue ahead. *Near here was found a pillar-stone inscribed in latin and ogham script to 'Similinus Tovisacus' – dating from*

3 Turn LEFT and go down the RIGHT fork of the forestry road, soon joined by another one. Shortly, when the road splits, take the RIGHT fork to follow a delightful green track – *with views of Llantisilio and Berwyn mountains* – soon passing a cottage. Continue down the track, then near the valley bottom, cross a stile on the right opposite a waymark post. Drop down half-LEFT to cross a footbridge over a stream, and go on over a stile. Go across the next field and over a stile in the far corner onto a road. Turn RIGHT into Clocaenog.

WALK 5

CWM ALWEN

DESCRIPTION A 7-mile walk (**A**) exploring the attractive wooded Alwen valley and its adjoining low hills, lying between the communities of Llanfihangel Glyn Myfyr and Pentre-Llyn Cymmer, featuring pleasant riverside walking, good views and an iron-age fort. Allow about 3½ hours. The route includes a shorter 4½ mile walk (**B**).

START Llanfihangel Glyn Myfyr [SH 987496]

DIRECTIONS From Cerrigydrudion, take the B5105 towards Ruthin, and after descending the steep hill into Llanfihangel, turn left on a minor road just before the bridge and the Crown Inn. Continue along the road, past the church and shortly you will reach three riverside picnic parking areas, just before the school.

L lanfihangel Glyn Myfyr was the birthplace of Owain Myfyr (Owen Jones) in 1749, a successful London businessman, with an interest in old Welsh manuscripts. His collection formed the basis of the 'Myfyrian Archaiology of Wales' published with his help.

1 Walk back along the road near the river, soon passing St. Michael's church – *which was flooded to a height of 9 feet in 1781* – to reach the B5105. Turn LEFT over the splendid single arched stone bridge carrying the road over the Afon Alwen and past the Crown Inn – *an old drovers inn.* Continue up the right hand side of the road and just before the second bend, cross a waymarked stile on the left. Go ahead a few yards, then swing half-RIGHT to follow a rising path up through the trees above a stream to reach lush open pasture. Continue up the field edge near the stream to cross a stile in the corner. *Pause to look back at the extensive views your short climb has achieved.* Cross a stony track and go half-LEFT over rough ground to pass a waymark post at the corner of a small plantation. Continue round the left hand edge of a small lake, passing beneath a small rocky escarpment. Keep on

with the waymarked path through the left hand side of a wettish reedy area, soon passing a small pool, and on to cross a stile in the fence ahead. Continue across the next two fields passing beneath Foel farm to reach a lane. Turn LEFT along the lane.

2 When the lane passes between two large stone buildings, climb the slope ahead to cross a hidden stile by the roof of the left building. Now go half-LEFT and on alongside the boundary fence – *with superb views from the Berwyns in the south to Arenig Fawr in the west* – to go through a gate onto a forestry track. Follow it LEFT. The track goes along the eastern edge of Cwm Alwen providing panoramic views. After a while the track swings sharp right and rises to a crossroad of forestry tracks. Here, turn LEFT and follow the track to a road by two houses. Turn LEFT and follow the road down to the river Alwen – *a pleasant place for a break. (For **Walk B**, retrace your steps and about 20 yards from the bridge, turn right into a green track. Follow it along the forest edge parallel with the river below. At the forest end cross a gate, and continue near the river. After crossing a stile, go through the trees to cross the river by a delightful old footbridge to the road. Follow it left back to the start.)*

3 For **Walk A** continue along up the road, then swing RIGHT along the access lane to Caer Ddunod. Go past the house and on with the lane to go through a gate in front of a white farmhouse, standing beneath the ramparts of Caer Ddunod iron-age fort. Go half-LEFT and follow a waymarked path through two gates to pass between outbuildings, and on along an enclosed track. At its end, cross a stile and walk along the bottom edge of the fort, before crossing a reedy area to drop down to the river Alwen. Continue by the river beneath the wooded slopes, over a stile, and along an open stretch of river, soon passing stepping stones leading to a house opposite. About 150 yards further, after crossing over a stream, go half-LEFT across open pasture to cross a stile just beyond the bend of the river. Continue across the field, over another stile, then go half-LEFT across open pasture, and on along

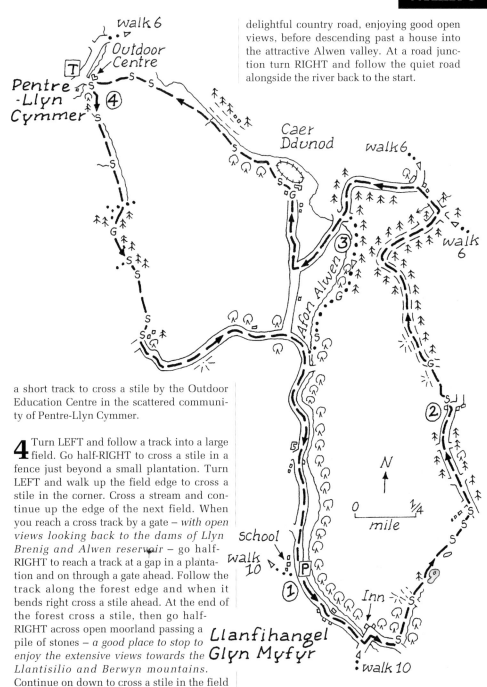

delightful country road, enjoying good open views, before descending past a house into the attractive Alwen valley. At a road junction turn RIGHT and follow the quiet road alongside the river back to the start.

a short track to cross a stile by the Outdoor Education Centre in the scattered community of Pentre-Llyn Cymmer.

4 Turn LEFT and follow a track into a large field. Go half-RIGHT to cross a stile in a fence just beyond a small plantation. Turn LEFT and walk up the field edge to cross a stile in the corner. Cross a stream and continue up the edge of the next field. When you reach a cross track by a gate – *with open views looking back to the dams of Llyn Brenig and Alwen reservoir* – go half-RIGHT to reach a track at a gap in a plantation and on through a gate ahead. Follow the track along the forest edge and when it bends right cross a stile ahead. At the end of the forest cross a stile, then go half-RIGHT across open moorland passing a pile of stones – *a good place to stop to enjoy the extensive views towards the Llantisilio and Berwyn mountains.* Continue on down to cross a stile in the field corner and follow a green track to reach the bend of a road. Turn LEFT and follow the

9

WALK 6
CRAIG BRON-BANOG

Pentre -Llyn Cymmer

Caer Ddur

DESCRIPTION A 8-mile figure of eight walk exploring the afforested undulating countryside south east of Llyn Brenig, on paths, forestry tracks and quiet lanes. The route meanders through Clocaenog forest, passing a hidden waterfall and ancient standing stone, to its highest point – Craig Bron-Banog at 1610 feet – offering panoramic views. It finishes with a delightful walk along a section of the Alwen river valley, passing by an iron-age hillfort. Allow about 4 hours. It can easily be shortened to a 3¼ mile walk.
START Pentre-Llyn Cymmer [SH 974527]
DIRECTIONS Pentre-Llyn Cymmer, a small scattered farming community, lies east just off the Cerrigydrudion – Llyn Brenig B4501 road. Go through the village, and a few hundred yards beyond the telephone box, there is a small roadside parking area on the right opposite a farm.

1 Continue along the road, over the river Alwen and past a house. After the road bends left round a cottage, take a waymarked path on the RIGHT, rising through the trees to reach a forestry track by Cefn Gors cottage. Cross the track and take the waymarked path opposite, soon crossing an old wall corner. Continue with the path through a young plantation to drop down to a forestry road. Follow it RIGHT, soon skirting upland pasture. As the road begins to swing left, turn RIGHT through a gateway along a stony track. About 20 yards after the track swings right, turn LEFT and follow a path dropping gently down through the trees, soon swinging LEFT alongside a fence and on down to cross a delightful small stone bridge over a river. Follow the path up to a forestry road. Turn RIGHT. *Down to your right is one of the highlights of the walk – a beautiful stepped waterfall set amongst the conifers in a deep side valley. If the river is in spate, this makes a wonderful sight.* Now take the LEFT fork of the forestry road to reach the bend of a road at a prominent viewpoint.

2 Continue ahead along the road to drop down to pass between houses. (*For the* **shorter** *walk continue with the road, resuming text at* **point** 4). Here, by Tal y Cefn Isaf, turn LEFT on a track to reach a crossroad of forestry roads. Turn RIGHT. After a while, the forestry road runs along the top edge of Cwm Alwen, providing panoramic views, before swinging LEFT to a road. Go ahead along the road, soon passing wall-enclosed upland pasture and old hillfarm – *with extensive views south over the forest.* The road then becomes enclosed by forest. (*After a few hundred yards, a track on the left, angling back into the forest, provides a short cut if required*). Continue along the road. After passing a track on your right, the road rises steadily. Shortly after the road levels out – *with views ahead of Llantisilio and Berwyn mountains* – turn LEFT by the old standing stone of Maen Cred – *discovered and re-erected by the Forestry Commision in June 1991* – onto a forestry road (½ *mile to the east is an iron-age village*). When it splits, keep straight ahead to reach a crossroads by a Mynydd Hiraethog trail waymark post.

3 Continue up the track ahead, and at another waymark post, swing RIGHT with the track up onto the open heather-covered top of Craig Bron-Banog with its transmitter mast. *A noticeboard advises that the other structures are part of an international project on the effects of climate change in heathlands. Do not enter the research area, but enjoy the stunning views: east over Clocaenog Forest to the Clwydian Hills;*

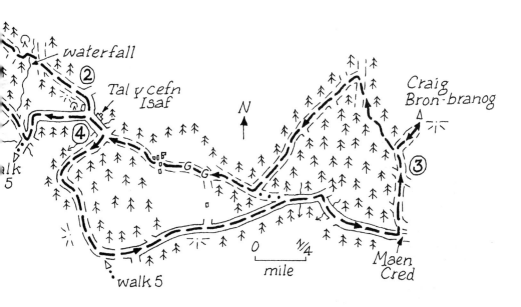

south east to the Llantisilio Mountains; south west and west to the mountains of Snowdonia; north over Mynydd Hiraethog. Return to the waymark post. Turn RIGHT to follow a path to a forestry track. Follow it RIGHT, and at the next track junction, turn LEFT. After about ¾ mile you will reach a forestry track T- junction. Turn RIGHT and at a crossroad of forestry tracks, turn LEFT. At the end of the forest go through a gate ahead, and follow a track down to pass through a farm and on along its access track. At a familiar crossroads, continue ahead to rejoin the road by Tal y Cefn Isaf. Turn LEFT.

4 Follow the road down and just before a bridge over the river Alwen, swing sharp RIGHT along a forestry road. Follow it along the attractive Alwen valley by the edge of the forest, passing the site of the iron-age fort of Caer Ddunod on the opposite bank of the river, then Ddol uchaf, and on to join your outward route at a road.

Maen Cred

WALK 7

LLYN BRENIG

DESCRIPTION A popular 10½ mile way-marked circuit of Llyn Brenig. The walk crosses the dam of the reservoir, before following a track along its eastern shores, passing sites of historical interest, before taking a path across Gors Maen Llwyd Nature Reserve at the northern end of the lake. It then follows a road meandering through the afforested western side of Llyn Brenig. Allow about 4 hours. Other shorter walks by Llyn Brenig include an archaelogical trail (see **Walk 8**) and a Nature Trail (leaflet available from the Centre).

START Llyn Brenig Visitor Centre [SH 968547]

DIRECTIONS Llyn Brenig lies just east of the B4501 Cerrigydrudion-Denbigh road, and is well signposted.

*L*lyn Brenig was first proposed as part of a twin reservoir scheme at the end of the 19thC by the then Corporation of Birkenhead to supply water direct to the town, but only Alwen reservoir was built. When Llyn Brenig was finally constructed between 1973-1976, its purpose was to regulate the flow of the river Dee, providing water for homes and industries in north-east Wales. It is 2⅓ miles long and 148 feet at its deepest point. It lies over 1200 feet above sea-level, with a climate that is wetter (average rainfall of 52 inches) and 2 – 3 degrees colder than at the coast.

The lake attracts many birds – including great crested grebe, cormorant, and heron, wintering mallard, teal and goldeneye and in spring, willow warblers return. The lake contains brown and locally reared rainbow trout and supports fly fishing, windsurfing, sailing and canoeing.

The Visitor Centre contains a shop, cafe and an interesting exhibition.

1 From the southern end of the Centre drop down to the jetty and walk along the lakeside. Go through a small gate and follow a path above the lake, then swing LEFT to walk across the dam. At its end, swing LEFT along a track. Keep with the main track as it

winds its way along the eastern shore of Llyn Brenig, passing through a forest and on by the edge of pastureland/moorland. *Prominent on the skyline to the north west is the remains of Gwylfa Hiraethog, the former shooting lodge of the first Viscount Devonport, a politician and first chairman of the Port of London Authority. It was built in 1913 to replace a wooden lodge, made in Norway and erected at 1,627 feet on the moors in the early 1890's. It was an impressive large stone building designed by Sir Edwin Cooper, a notable architect, and had commanding views. It was used as a residence for family and guests, including Lloyd George, during the grouse-shooting season until 1925, when it was sold. The family travelled in a special railway coach from London to Denbigh, where they enjoyed refreshments at the Crown Hotel, before continuing their journey by horse wagon. Sadly it is now a ruin. A notable landmark on the Denbigh moors, often referred to as the 'Haunted House', it has featured in several films.* The track loops inland to pass near Hafotty Sion Llwyd – *once a home for shepherds or bailiffs* – to reach a Bronze Age Ring Cairn and burial mound. Continue along the track to reach a car park and toilets.

2 Continue up the lane and after about ⅓ mile, at a waymark post, go half-LEFT to follow the waymarked trail as it meanders across Gors Maen Llwyd Nature Reserve, passing near the old standing stone of Maen Llwyd. *Managed by the North Wales Wildlife Trust since 1988, the Reserve consists of heather moorland and peat bog, rich in plant and insects, which in turn support many small birds – eg. skylark, stonechat, and whinchat. The moorland habitat is particularly important for the increasingly rare Red and Black Grouse. Selective burning of heather, encouraging young shoots on which they feed, is helping to maintain these important species.* After a while, the path runs alongside the road before heading half-LEFT through a clump of trees and rising gently through heather.

3 At a path junction by a waymark post, turn RIGHT back towards the road, then follow a green track, which runs by or near the road, passing a parking area at Bryn Maen. *This track is the old road from Pentrefoelas to Denbigh, which was replaced in 1826 by the turnpike road, now the A543. Near Bryn Maen once stood a cottage occupied in the 19thC by a reputed miser with a hoard of golden sovereigns, who had seven locks on his door. Legend tells that after heavy snow, he discovered the remains of his elderly neighbour half eaten by her cat!* The track gradually deteriorates, leaving the road to run alongside a forest. After going through a gate, continue on a track through the forest to join a road at a clearing.

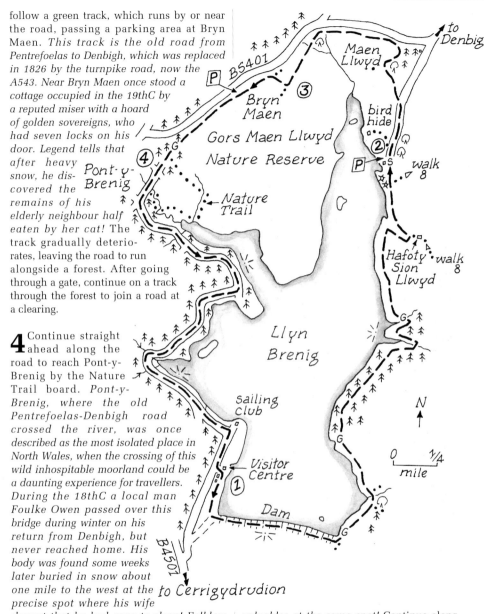

4 Continue straight ahead along the road to reach Pont-y-Brenig by the Nature Trail board. *Pont-y-Brenig, where the old Pentrefoelas-Denbigh road crossed the river, was once described as the most isolated place in North Wales, when the crossing of this wild inhospitable moorland could be a daunting experience for travellers. During the 18thC a local man Foulke Owen passed over this bridge during winter on his return from Denbigh, but never reached home. His body was found some weeks later buried in snow about one mile to the west at the precise spot where his wife dreamt that he had gone to sleep! Folklore also tells of a young man who met a mysterious stranger dressed in grey clothes with gold buttons here. The stranger smiled, jumped off the bridge and vanished into the bog. Each time the young man passed that way he found a small pile of money and valuables at the same spot!* Continue along the road, past an exit road, and on along the western side of the lake. The road passes cleared sections of forest giving good views of the lake, then another exit road and the sailing club to eventually reach the Centre.

WALK 8
ON THE TRAIL OF OUR ANCESTORS

DESCRIPTION This 2½ mile walk follows a waymarked Archaelogical Trail established by the Welsh Water Authority through undulating upland pasture adjoining Llyn Brenig on its north east side. It visits some of the important Bronze Age ceremonial and burial sites, and other places of archaelogical interest investigated between 1973 and 1975 during the construction of Llyn Brenig, and offers extensive views. A more detailed leaflet is available from the Visitor Centre. Containing a shorter option, the main trail crosses open reedy, occasionally wet ground, and is best undertaken in good weather. Allow about 2 hours.

START Archaelogical trail car park, Llyn Brenig (N.E.) [SH 984574]

DIRECTIONS From the A543 Pentrefoelas – Denbigh road, take the B4501 towards Cerrigydrudion/Llyn Brenig. After 1 mile turn left towards Nantglyn. After about 1½ miles, turn right by a recreational board to follow a lane down to a car park and toilets by the lake.

1 Cross a stile by a gate to the left of the toilets. *A nearby information board sets the scene.* Walk along the stony lakeside road to soon reach the Ring Cairn (**A**). *The low stone ring surrounded by a circle of posts served as a ceremonial monument from about 1680 BC. Later it was used as a cremation burial site.* Now visit the nearby mound of Boncyn Arian (**B**). *Boncyn Arian is a large Bronze Age burial mound covering a central grave used about 2000 BC. Nearby is the site of a Mesolithic camp dating from around 5000 BC. once occupied by Stone Age hunters.* Return to the road and cross a stile by a gate. Now go half-LEFT up open pasture to a waymark post and on through a reedy area to reach the Hafotai Settlement (**C**). *Dating from the 16thC, sever-*

al stone huts, probably thatched with heather and rushes, once occupied both sides of the stream. They served as summer dwellings for the people who brought their animals to graze on the moors. (For a **shorter** *walk, simply follow the nearby stream down to cross a stile by the start.)*

2 The waymarked trail heads south near the edge of the forest – *offering panoramic views of Llyn Brenig and, on a clear day, the mountains of Snowdonia.* It then drops down to cross a stile near a gate at the forest corner. Cross a stream, and go up the slope ahead, past a waymark post, and on up the reed covered slope. At another waymark post, swing RIGHT to reach the impressive stone Platform Cairn (**D**) at a prominent viewpoint. *Built around 2000 B.C. on an earlier site occupied by Bronze Age man, the cairn contained two cremation burials – one the remains of an adult and child placed in an urn beneath a large stone.*

3 From the waymark post near the platform, go east for about 40 yards, then swing RIGHT to reach an information board overlooking Hen Ddinbych (**E**). *The rectangular enclosure contains the stone foundations of a large medieval farmhouse, and evidence of other buildings.* Drop down to cross

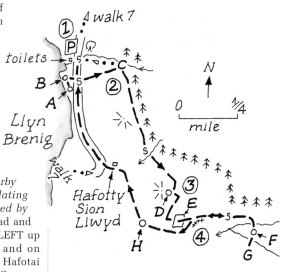

the site and on to a waymark post by a fence corner. The path now runs parallel with the fence on your right, before crossing a stile by a gate in the fence corner. Turn LEFT and go past a waymark post to skirt the bottom end of an area of bracken. After about 300 yards, swing RIGHT across the heather covered flat side valley, over a stream, and on to reach a Bronze Age kerb-cairn (**F**) by a white marker post. *The wooden posts mark the post-holes of a possible prehistoric hut, over which the cairn containing a cremation burial was built.* Nearby is Maen Cleddau (**G**) – *a large glacial stone, reputed to have been broken by a giant's sword.* Retrace your steps to the waymark post by the fence corner at Hen Ddinbych.

4 Now go half-LEFT to skirt round the southern end of Hen Ddinbych and up the slope to another Bronze Age kerb-cairn (**H**). From here head half-RIGHT, soon dropping down the hillside on a track leading to Hafotty Sion Llwyd. *Rebuilt in 1881 using stone from Hen Ddinbych and other sites, this was the home of shepherds or bailiffs.* Pass in front of the house and on to follow the lakeside road back to the start.

WALK 9

ALWEN RESERVOIR

DESCRIPTION This easy 2¼ mile walk provides close views of the scenic reservoir and a taste of the forest that surrounds it. Allow about 1½ hours.

START The dam, Alwen Reservoir. [SH 956530]

DIRECTIONS Go past the turning to Llyn Brenig Centre on the B4501 towards Cerrigydrudion, then midway down a hill before the turning to Pentre-Llyn Cymmer, turn right along a stony track – by an Alwen Reservoir recreational board. Soon take the left fork, and after passing between houses, turn left to park by the impressive dam of the early 20thC Alwen reservoir – built to supply water to Birkenhead.

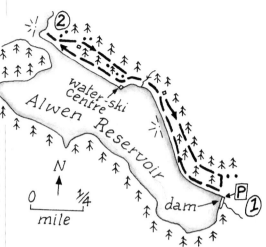

1 Go onto to the dam for a good view along the reservoir. Retrace your steps, and at the end of the dam, turn LEFT and go through a gate by a waymark post (Pen-y-Ffrith). Follow the lakeside path, at first on a green track, then alongside the edge of a plantation to join a forestry track by a stone house. Follow the track LEFT and when it splits, go half-LEFT down to the Water Ski Training Centre. Turn RIGHT on a path passing above the building, and follow it along the forest edge above the reservoir. At the end of the forest, continue near the old iron fence to its corner – *with a good view across the narrow central section of the reservoir towards the high moorland ridge of Mwdwl-eithin.*

2 Retrace your steps for about 20 yards to where a stone wall meets the iron fence. Go through a gap in the fence and follow a path up alongside the wall to reach a forestry road just above. Follow it RIGHT past a ruin. Keep with the RIGHT fork, with glimpses of the lake through the trees, soon rejoining your outward route. Now simply follow the road past the house you met earlier and through the forest back to the start.

WALK 10
CAER CARADOG

DESCRIPTION A 5¼ mile walk (**A**) through a little visited area of open countryside and upland pasture, with excellent views. The route explores the attractive open undulating countryside west of Cwm Alwen, visits a small reservoir, later rising across the slopes of Y Drum to the site of Caer Caradog, an iron-age hillfort. It then follows an old drovers' route, which contours around the mid-slopes of Mwdwl-eithin, before dropping down to Llanfihangel. A shorter 2½ mile walk (**B**) is included. Allow about 3 hours.
START Llanfihangel Glyn Myfyr [SH 987496] See **Walk 5**.

1 Walk along the road towards the school, then turn LEFT through a gate opposite a childrens play area. Follow a rising green track past the end of the school playground and on alongside a stream. When the track splits, swing RIGHT over the stream and through a gate. Now go half-LEFT up the field to join a green track. Follow it LEFT through a gate, and on through an abandoned farm. Soon swing LEFT with the track over the stream, then RIGHT and follow the track to go through the top right hand corner of the field. Continue with the enclosed track for 20 yards, then swing half-LEFT through a gap in the gorse boundary, and go up the field to pass through a gate in the top corner. Go through a gap in the old wall just ahead, and walk alongside the fence/wall on your left to go through a gate near the corner. Turn RIGHT. (*For* **Walk B**, *follow a gated green track heading south, and on with a lane to turn left along the B5105. After a few hundred yards go through a gate on the right onto a green track. Follow the track, then lane to a road. Follow it left down into Llanfinghafel.*)

2 For **Walk A** go through the higher gate. Turn LEFT and go across open pasture to cross a stile alongside a barn by a rock escarpment. Go on to cross a gate just beyond a ruined cottage. Go half-LEFT to see the unexpected sight of a small attractive rowan tree edged reservoir – *home for wildfowl and a quiet spot for fishing*. Retrace your steps, and after crossing the gate by the cottage, go half-RIGHT to pass through the nearest gate. Walk towards another old cottage, and after about 80 yards, turn LEFT to go through a gate. Turn RIGHT along the field edge, passing the old smallholding, to reach a lane. Follow it LEFT, past Maes Tyddyn farm, and on – *with good open views* – to reach the B5105. Turn RIGHT down the road.

3 After a few hundred yards, turn LEFT through a gate to pass between an old house and its outbuilding, over a stream, and on through a gate. Continue up an enclosed old green track. After crossing a stream, it swings half-RIGHT and rises steadily across the open western slopes of Y Drum – *offering excellent views west towards Cerrigydrudion and beyond the hills and mountains of Snowdonia*. When the track deteriorates through a wettish section, and just beyond a small section of collapsed wall, go through a gateway ahead. Now follow the fence on your right, cross another gate, and keep on with the fence, soon passing the distinctive ramparts of Caer Caradog hillfort. *Situated at 1250' on a hillock on the western flanks of Y Drum, occupying a strategic position over important valley routes, the iron-age fort has a circular rampart of earth and shale enclosing an area of about 2 acres. It is reputed to be the legendary fortified base of King Caractacus, who was captured by the Romans and taken in chains to Rome. Beyond on a hilltop is a solitary wind turbine.* Cross a gate and at the fence corner, continue ahead, passing to the right of a small depression, and on to drop down to go through a gate onto a lane. Turn LEFT and at a road junction, continue ahead, soon passing the entrance to Ty Hen. Just beyond the next farm, when the lane bends left, go straight ahead to follow a delightful enclosed old drovers track towards the green hill of Mwdwl-eithin.

4 After going through a gate at the end of the track, swing half-LEFT past a Mynndd Hiraethog trail waymark post to follow the track alongside a wall up the open

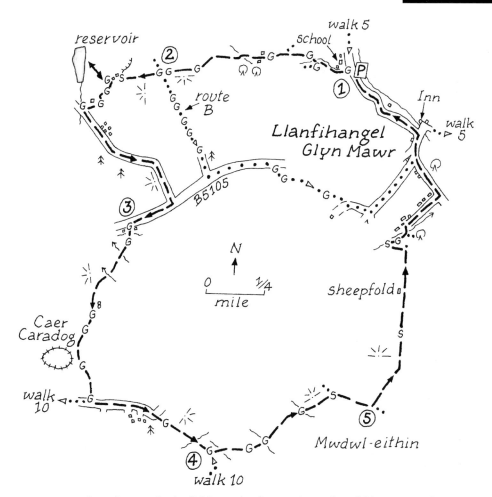

pasture to go through a gate in the field corner. Continue ahead, through another gate, and on with the track to contour round the open slopes of Mwdwl-eithin. *About 100 yards beyond another gate a small section of wall makes an ideal place to stop to take in the views.* When the track swings down left, cross a stile ahead, and follow another green track running between the green upland pasture and the higher heather and bracken covered slopes.

5 Just before a gate by a waymark post, swing LEFT and begin a gradual descent towards Llanfihangel. Cross a ladder-stile, and continue ahead alongside the fence.

After passing a sheepfold, continue down a gorse enclosed green track, and at its end, turn LEFT down the field edge to cross a stile at the bottom. Turn RIGHT, go through a gate, and on alongside a stream. Soon cross the stream by a red barn, go past a farm and along its access lane. At a road junction, turn LEFT along the road into Llanfihangel. At the next junction, turn RIGHT to reach the B5105. Cross the road and follow it RIGHT for perhaps a drink at the Crown Inn – *a traditional pub with a scenic beer garden above the river* – or, turn LEFT along the minor road, soon passing St. Michael's church, back to the start.

WALK 11

AROUND CWM CEIRW

DESCRIPTION A 8½ mile walk exploring the remote hills and valleys lying between the ancient communities of Llangwm and Cerrigydrudion, offering extensive views. The route rises from Llangwm to high upland pasture above the Ceirw valley, then follows an old drovers' route down to Cerrigydrudion, passing the site of an iron-age fort. It then rises through open country to a prominent wind turbine, before descending into side valleys, and on past an ancient manor house back to Llangwm. Allow about 5 hours.

START Llangwm [SH 966446] or alternative Cerrigydrudion [SH 954488].

DIRECTIONS From Cerrigydrudion, take the A5 towards Corwen, then turn right on a minor road to Llangwm. Park tidily by the former village church. See Walk 9 for the alternative start.

*L*langwm is reputed to be the site of a battle in the 10thC when the Prince of South Wales was slain by the Prince of North Wales. Traditionally an agricultural community, where cattle/sheep were fattened before drovers moved them to London markets it was once noted for its large black cattle fair held on 18th April. It also once produced knitted stockings which were sold in London and Liverpool markets.

1 Walk back through the village. After crossing the Afon Medrad, swing RIGHT with the road and after about 150 yards, take a waymarked Mynydd Hiraethog path on the left. Go up through a small wood, then, go half-LEFT, over a track, and on to cross a stile in the corner. Drop down to turn LEFT through a gate at the end of a barn. Go RIGHT through another gate and on down the farm's access track, soon passing a chapel, to reach a road. Go through the gate opposite and drop down to walk alongside the river Ceirw, and on over a footbridge. Follow an enclosed path to the A5. Turn

LEFT, and after 25 yards cross the road and follow the waymarked path through a farm to go through a gate at the right-hand side of the house. Now follow a wide green track that rises steadily up the part-wooded hillside. At its end continue up the field edge. After about 150 yards, turn LEFT over a stile, and go along the field edge, passing a small plantation, to go through a gate by a large barn.

2 Continue along a waymarked track passing to the right of the large farm. At a wider track follow it RIGHT – *with new views towards Snowdonia and Caer Caradog fort clearly visible on the other side of the valley.* After a second stile on the track, go half-RIGHT on a green track and through the right of two gates. Ignore the track rising right, but continue ahead by the wall to go through a gate in the corner. Now go half-LEFT with the wall, and after crossing a stile, swing LEFT down to a waymark post. Here you leave the Mynydd Hiraethog trail by turning LEFT through a gate and following a delightful enclosed old drovers' track up to a road. Go along the road ahead past two farms.

3 At a junction continue ahead, soon passing close to Caer Caradog iron-age fort just up to your right (see **Walk 7**). Continue with this quiet upland road – *an old drovers' route offering superb views.* It steadily descends. At Felin Bwlch turn LEFT along a track, soon passing a house to enter a small discreet caravan site. Leave it by a kissing gate to continue along the edge of two fields, past a barn, and down a track into Cerrigydrudion. Go ahead to reach the A5. Cross the road and turn RIGHT, soon passing a cafe and The Saracens Head. *Note the old milestone. Holyhead, Corwen – but where is Cernioge? See **Walk 14** for the answer.*

4 Turn LEFT along a road signposted to Cwmpenanner. At a junction, turn LEFT past Pen-y-Bryn Bach. Soon the road heads across open country towards a wind turbine on the skyline. Just after passing a farm on your right, as the road begins to descend, go through a gate by a waymark post. Go across the field, over a stile and along the field edge to reach a ruined cottage. Here, turn LEFT, go through a gate, and on to cross a footbridge over the Afon Ceirw. Turn RIGHT and go through the bottom edge of the next three fields and through a narrow strip of woodland. Continue ahead to cross a fence by a large stone 40 yards above

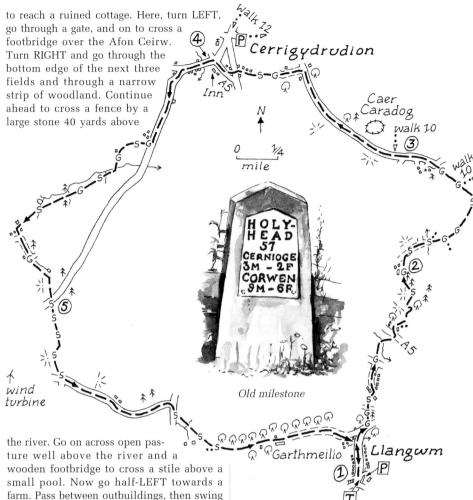

Old milestone

the river. Go on across open pasture well above the river and a wooden footbridge to cross a stile above a small pool. Now go half-LEFT towards a farm. Pass between outbuildings, then swing LEFT up to join and follow the farm's access lane. At a bend by a stone building, go through the middle of three gates and walk up the right bank of the stream and on to reach an old field embankment/fence. Follow the boundary RIGHT to reach a road (*stiles have been requested*). Turn RIGHT.

5 Cross a stile on your left to join the Mynydd Hiraethog trail back to Llangwm. Go half-RIGHT up two fields, then skirt the left hand side of a reedy area, before swinging RIGHT beneath the higher rock escarpment to cross a stile. Just ahead is the wind turbine. Turn LEFT along the field edge to a

road. Follow it LEFT down to the B4501 then turn RIGHT. After 100 yards, go LEFT over a stile and follow the fence down and round to cross a stile in the field corner. Now go slightly RIGHT away from the wall to gradually drop down to cross a stile by the bottom corner of a wood. Turn LEFT and follow the track along the wood edge, passing Gamekeepers Cottage and Garthmeilio – *an impressive country estate house, dating from the 14thC*. Continue along its access track. At a bend, take the RIGHT fork to soon reach the road. Turn RIGHT back to the start.

WALK 12

CRAIG YR IYRCHEN

DESCRIPTION A 6½ mile walk exploring attractive upland pasture and moorland fringes north of Cerrigydrudion, rising in stages to a height of over 1400 feet with excellent views. The route crosses lower pastures, then rises very steadily up a quiet lane, before following a waymarked path across the upper slopes of Craig yr Iyrchen. It then descends to the ancient hamlet of Cefn Brith, before returning by road and field paths. Allow about 3½ hours. The route also offers a simple 1¼ walk.

START Cerrigydrudion [SH 954488]

DIRECTIONS Cerrigydrudion lies just off the A5. There is a signposted car park alongside a garage at the beginning of Ruthin Road (B5105)

*C*errigydrudion is the largest settlement in Mynydd Hiraethog. Its name meaning 'the stones of the daring ones' is reputedly a reference to a large pile of stones once located near the church. Local tradition says that they were the prison in which Cyn-vrig Rwth, a lawless chieftain, kept his captives. The original 18thC London–Holyhead turnpike coach road once passed through the village centre, but in the early 19thC, Thomas Telford diverted the route, building a new road from Cerrigydrudion to Glasfryn, now the A5. Much of the surrounding grazing land was let to Anglesey dealers for fattening up their cattle on the way to the Midland markets. The village was an important shoeing station and one of its famous sons was the 17thC drover and poet, Edward Morus – still droving at 82! In the 19thC villagers were involved in cattle/sheep breeding, spinning of woollen yarn and knitting of stockings. There used to be five fairs a year. In 1854, George Borrow, the eminent traveller and writer of 'Wild Wales' stayed at 'the Lion – whether the white, black, red or green Lion I do not know' after walking 20 miles from Llangollen on his way to Bangor. Here he enjoyed good conversation with a doctor and

a Welsh-speaking Italian. In the centre stands St. Mary Magdalene's church, dating from the16thC and restored in 1874, and almshouses built in 1716.

1 Walk along Ruthin Road to reach the driveway to Bwlch-y-beudy at the outskirts of Cerrigydrudion. *On the skyline beyond the white cottage ahead are the distinctive ramparts of Caer Caradog iron-age hillfort.* Turn LEFT up the driveway, then cross a ladder-stile on the left by a waymark post. Walk ahead along the field edge to cross another ladder-stile in the corner – *enjoying good views over Cerrigydrudion. Note the single wind turbine on the skyline.* Continue along the edge of the next three fields to reach the B4501. Go along the road ahead towards Cefn Brith, soon passing a waymarked path on the left – the short/return route. Continue along the road.

2 After passing the entrance track to Ty-tan-y-graig, turn RIGHT at a road junction and go up the minor road. After a while it levels out to provide panoramic views west along the wide river valley towards the mountains of Snowdonia. This delightful walled enclosed road winds up the hillside, past a side road and a house. At the next junction keep ahead. The enclosed road ends at the entrance drive to Ty'n-y-gilfach. Continue ahead with a more open lane across high upland pasture grazed by sheep – *soon with new views east towards Clocaenog Forest and ahead to the plantation around the hidden Alwen reservoir, with a glimpse of the dam tower among the trees.*

3 When you reach Craig-yr-iyrchen-fawr, turn LEFT over a waymarked stile and follow a rising stony track. *Across the treetops to the north, visible on the skyline, is the ruin of Gwylfa Hiraethog – the former shooting lodge of Viscount Devonport (For details see* **Walk 7**). After about 250 yards, just before the track ends in a small quarry, and by a waymark post, go half-LEFT to follow a waymarked rising path above the quarry and across moorland to go over a stile in a fence. *Here look back for a view of Alwen reservoir.* Go half-LEFT to reach another

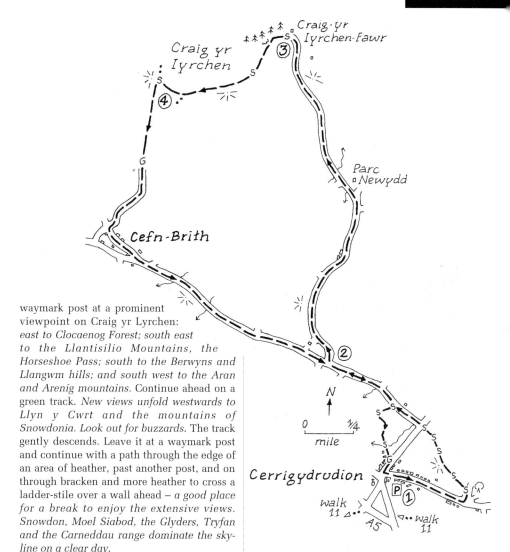

waymark post at a prominent viewpoint on Craig yr Lyrchen: *east to Clocaenog Forest; south east to the Llantisilio Mountains, the Horseshoe Pass; south to the Berwyns and Llangwm hills; and south west to the Aran and Arenig mountains.* Continue ahead on a green track. *New views unfold westwards to Llyn y Cwrt and the mountains of Snowdonia. Look out for buzzards.* The track gently descends. Leave it at a waymark post and continue with a path through the edge of an area of heather, past another post, and on through bracken and more heather to cross a ladder-stile over a wall ahead – *a good place for a break to enjoy the extensive views. Snowdon, Moel Siabod, the Glyders, Tryfan and the Carneddau range dominate the skyline on a clear day.*

4 Turn LEFT and follow a green track steadily descending the hillside. After going through a gate continue down an enclosed lane. At a crossroad, in the hamlet of Cefn Brith, turn LEFT, and at the next junction, continue ahead. Follow the quiet country road back towards Cerrigydrudion for about 1½ miles. *This was the route of the original 18thC turnpike road.* When you reach the waymarked path on the right

passed on your outward route, cross the stile, walk alongside the wall and go over a stile in the corner. Turn LEFT along the field edge and after going through a gateway in the corner, turn RIGHT and drop down the field alongside the wall. Towards its end, swing half-LEFT to cross a stile by a stream. Go on up the field edge to reach the road opposite the school. Turn RIGHT to reach the centre of Cerrigydrudion.

WALK 13
CWM PENANNER

DESCRIPTION This 6½ mile walk explores a little-known area of upland pasture and the hidden attractive valley of Cwm Penanner with its scattered farming community. The route, which uses quiet country roads, field paths and a superb open upland bridleway, offers a great sense of space and excellent ever changing distant views. It can easily be shortened or varied, with additional link paths/road shown. Allow about 3½ hours.

START Crossroads above Cwm Penanner [SH 918480]

DIRECTIONS From Glasfryn, take the minor road heading south off the A5, opposite a pottery. Follow it past a side road to rise steadily up the hillside to reach the signposted Bala, Cerrigydrudion, Blaen Cwm, Glasfryn crossroads, where there is off-road parking.

1 Walk back along the road towards Glasfryn, and after nearly ⅓ mile, turn RIGHT through a gate by a footpath post. Go across the field to pass by a ruined cottage, over a stream and on to cross a waymarked stile in the fence corner. Now follow a stiled path through the edge of five fields – *apparently regularly walked by an elderly lady, the last occupant of the cottage, on her way to church in Cerrigydrudion* – to reach a road. Continue ahead along the road. After a few hundred yards, turn RIGHT through a way-marked gate opposite a small ruin. Ignore the track leading to a transmitter mast, but go half-RIGHT up across open ground and on down to a wall/old fence boundary corner by a gate – *offering your first view into the hidden Cwm Penanner, with the solitary wind-turbine on the high ridge, and the Llangwm hills beyond.* Continue alongside a fence on your left, then at a wall end, go slightly RIGHT away from the boundary to cross a stile by a sheepfold. Go on to pass to the left of a reedy area and on through a gate onto a farm's access lane. (*Improvements, including the installation of stiles, are due to take place on the next described section, which follows field paths to the road. An alternative is to turn right and follow quiet roads to point* **3**).

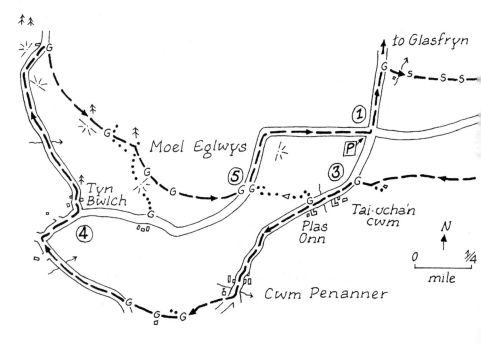

2 Turn LEFT and just before the farm, go through a gate on the right. Start along a green track, then follow the fence on the left. At its corner, continue ahead, then after 100 yards, drop down to cross a fence corner. Now follow the wall on your right, over an old stone stile, and on alongside the wall to cross the field corner ahead. Follow the boundary on your left to cross the remains of an old wall in the field corner, and the fence just ahead. The path goes through an area of gorse (*to be cut back*) to cross a fence into a large field. Head towards the right of a large farm in the mid-distance to cross a fence above a ruin, and go on to join and follow a rough track to the road Turn LEFT.

3 Follow the road past Tai-ucha'n-cwm. *Note the Lion 1720 datestone on the front of the house.* Continue along the road past Plas Onn. (*To shorten or vary the walk, go through a gate opposite the gable end of the house and follow a green track that winds its way up the hillside to a higher road at point* **5**.) Follow the road to steadily descend into Cwm Penanner to reach the chapel by the river and a road junction. *A signpost indicates that you are only a mere 7 miles from Bala! The chapel built in 1898 continues to serve this scattered community.* Continue along the road and at the corner of the church-yard, by a footpath post, leave the road and follow the boundary on your right through a reedy area. Soon the path swings away from the boundary to go through a

waymarked gate. Continue ahead, and after about 30 yards, when the path splits, take the LEFT fork to follow a delightful stone-paved path through another reedy area to go through a gate by a cottage. Continue ahead alongside an old field boundary, and when it bends right, keep ahead to go through a small wooden gate in the boundary ahead and on to rejoin the road. Follow the road up to a junction. Turn RIGHT and follow the road up to another junction.

4 Turn LEFT up past Tyn Bwlch. Follow the road for about ¾ mile beneath the eastern slopes of Garn Prys. The road begins to descend and swing right – *with the mountains of Snowdonia clearly visible to the north-west.* As the road becomes less steep, look for two gates on the right on a slight bend opposite a small fenced enclosure. Here turn sharp RIGHT through the higher gate and follow a rising green track. It soon levels out as it crosses upland pastureland and passes a small plantation. After going through a gate, keep ahead and after 50 yards when the track splits, continue ahead on the left fork, soon going over a cross-track and on up through a gate. This delightful green track – *a highlight of the walk* – contours round the higher slopes of Moel Eglwys – *offering panoramic views as far as the Berwyns and Arans* – before descending gently to the road.

5 Turn LEFT and follow this delightful high-level road contouring the eastern slopes of Moel Eglwys and high upland pasture back to the start, enjoying the excellent views.

Chapel in Cwm Penanner

WALK 14
LLYN Y CWRT

DESCRIPTION A 6½-mile walk (**A**) across the lower northern slopes of the wide Merddwr river valley between Glasfryn and Rhydlydan. The route features a small attractive hidden upland lake near the tiny hamlet of Cernioge, once an important staging point on the old London-Holyhead coach road, delightful old walled tracks and extensive views. Allow about 3½ hours. The route offers two shorter walks of 2 miles (**B**) and 4½ miles (**C**).
START Glasfryn [SH 917502]
DIRECTIONS Glasfryn lies on the A5 midway between Pentrefoelas and Cerrigydrudion. On entering the village from Pentrefoelas, just beyond a garage, park in a lay-by on the right. Note that car parking in the village is time restricted.

1 Walk east along the A5 through the village towards Cerrigydrudion. By the old school turn LEFT on a side road signposted to Cefn Brith. Follow this quiet country road for nearly ½ mile, and on a bend, cross a waymarked stile on the left to join the Mynydd Hiraethog trail. Head up the field to join a wall on the left. Continue by the wall along the field edge, over a footbridge and on over a stone stile in the field corner. Keep on along the field edge, over a ladder-stile, and on by an old green track – *enjoying extensive open views from the Berwyns in the southeast to the mountains of Snowdonia to the west. Also visible is Llyn y Cwrt.* After going through a metal gate continue ahead, now with the wall on your right, to reach a cross-road of walled tracks. (*For* **Walk B** *turn left.*)

2 Follow the enclosed track ahead, soon descending to cross a river, and on up to go through a gate by another track. Go through a gate ahead, and walk alongside the wall on your left, over a stream and a stile, and up the edge of the next field. After crossing a stile in a fence continue ahead along a small grassy ridge. *On a clear day, Moel Siabod, Snowdon, the Glyders, Tryfan and the Carneddau range dominate the skyline*

ahead. To your right is the high moorland ridge of Mwdwl-eithin. Pass a waymark post and drop down to a waymarked path junction post. Go on through a wall gap and over a stile. Follow the wall to reach another waymarked path junction post.

3 Here you leave the trail by turning LEFT over a gate. Follow a delightful walled track down to an old hill-farm. Pass between the house and outbuilding, then swing LEFT behind a corrugated shed and stone building to cross a fence into a field. Go ahead to cross a gate in the corner, over a stream, and on across the next field to cross an old stone stile in a wall corner by a wall gap. Go ahead a few yards, then swing RIGHT down the field edge alongside a wall – *with a good view of Llyn y Cwrt fringed by alder woodland.* Cross a gate in the field corner. Continue along the field edge, through a gate, and along a track to join the farm's access track. Follow it RIGHT almost to the A5 by Cernioge Mawr farm. *This was a well known coaching inn on the old London-Holyhead road, until its licence was transferred to the Foelas Arms Hotel in Pentrefoelas in 1839. This explains why 'Cernioge' appears on old milestones alongside towns such as Holyhead and Corwen. It had stabling for 69 horses, and provided the Duke of Wellington with his finest team of horses during a race against a friend to prove that the inland route to Holyhead was faster than a coastal route. In 1832, Victoria, aged 13, then heir to the throne, enjoyed tea here during her first visit to Wales. In 1854, George Borrow, the eminent traveller and writer passed by on his walk to Bangor and mused about its name.*

4 About 70 yards before the road, with a stone barn just ahead, turn LEFT along the wall to go through a gate in the wall corner. (*For* **Walk C** *simply walk along the pavement on the A5 for ½ mile back to the start.*) Swing LEFT up the edge of the field, cross a gate in the corner, and continue straight ahead to go through a gate at a wood corner ahead. Go along the edge of the wood to reach Llyn y Cwrt with its stone boathouse. Continue along the lake edge and go through a gate by its corner. Go through the next two

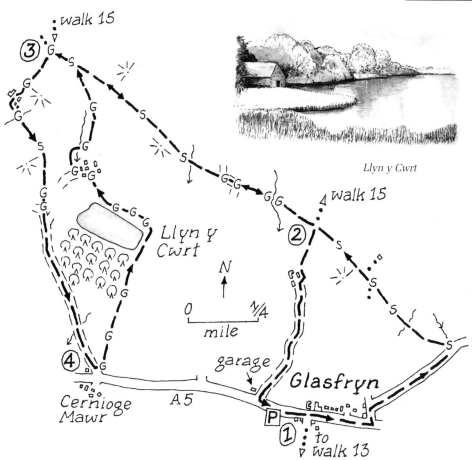

Llyn y Cwrt

fields, passing above the lake, and on across the third field to reach the wall ahead. Follow it RIGHT up to a farm and go through a gate in the field corner by the house. Bear LEFT through the farm then swing RIGHT through a gate up a track. Follow it through two further gates to reach the waymarked finger post passed earlier. Swing sharp RIGHT and return along your outward route until you reach the crossroad of walled tracks met at point **2**. Turn RIGHT and follow the enclosed track down to a house. Turn RIGHT through a gate at the end of the house, then swing LEFT and follow its access track to the A5 by the garage. Turn LEFT back to the start.

About the author, David Berry

David has lived in North Wales for nearly 30 years and greatly appreciates the beauty, culture and history of its landscape. He hopes that his comprehensive guides will encourage people to explore its diverse scenery and rich heritage. A keen walker and photographer, with an interest in local history, he is equally at home on a country ramble or on a mountain top. He has also undertaken many long distance walks, including coast to coast crossings of Wales, Scotland and England.

WALK 15
MWDWL-EITHIN

DESCRIPTION An exhilarating 8¼ mile walk around the remote high moorland ridge of Mwdwl-eithin lying between the A5 and the A543, offering excellent views. The route rises to cross the broad ridge at 1500 feet, then skirts its eastern slopes to descend to a side valley near the neck of the Alwen reservoir. It then follows an ancient track up to a bwlch, before descending across moorland and returning via field paths and tracks. *This moorland romp can be wet underfoot, and is for experienced, well equipped walkers only. It should be avoided in poor visibility.* Allow about 5 hours.
START Glasfryn [SH 917502] See **Walk 14**.

1 Follow the instructions contained in the first section of Walk 14.

2 Here you leave the trail by taking the enclosed track rising RIGHT up the hillside – *used by drovers to move cattle and sheep from upland pastures on their journey to distant markets.* At its end pass through sheepfolds to reach open upland country. Continue along the edge of a small grassy ridge, passing to the left of a reedy area. After about 200 yards, swing LEFT with a green track. Take its LEFT fork, faint at first, but soon more distinct, to ford a stream. Now swing RIGHT to follow a clear path parallel with an old wall on your left. After crossing a stream, keep the increasingly sparse remains of the wall on your left, to go through a gate in a more substantial wall.

3 Go straight ahead through a reedy area, over a cross-path, and about 100 yards from the gate, follow a clear path rising gently up the heather covered southern slopes of Mwdwl-eithin ahead. As you get higher, the path becomes more intermittent as it passes just to the right of a bracken covered slope on which stand two small trees. Go on through a grassy area to pass about 250 yards left of a cluster of stones set among the heather on the skyline ahead, where the gradient lessens. Continue ahead along the edge

of heather covered high ground to your left. Soon the ground levels out – *with good views across to the summit cairns on Mwdwl-eithin and beyond the mountains stretching from the Nantle ridge, through Snowdon to the Carneddau range.*

4 Here, follow a path skirting a heather covered small top to your right to pass over the broad ridge – *with views across to Alwen reservoir and its surrounding forest. Prominent on the distant skyline is the ruined shooting lodge of Gwylfa Hiraethog* (see **Walk 7**). Follow the clear path heading north as it first contours, then steadily descends across the bracken and heather covered eastern slopes of Mwdwl-eithin. It then crosses a level wet reedy area. After passing above a small ruin continue in the same direction across drier moorland – *with the Alwen reservoir becoming increasingly revealed to your gaze* – to eventually cross a gate in a fence – *with a view of Llyn Aled.*

5 Now head down towards a solitary tree in a side valley in line with the footbridge over the neck of the Alwen. After crossing the remains of an old fence, swing RIGHT down to a most unexpected sight – a waymark post just beyond a stream. Turn LEFT and go past sheepfolds to reach the tree by a ruin. *Continue ahead on an old track – the remains of the old Denbigh – Pentrefoelas road, which was replaced by a turnpike road, now the A543, in 1826.* Follow it up the hillside, passing through a gate. When you reach level ground – *with extensive views towards Llyn Alwen and the mountains of Snowdonia beyond* – swing half-LEFT along the wide flat reedy ridge overlooking the A543 on the faint line of the old track to go through a gate on the skyline ahead. *Set amongst the expansive moorland landscape are three lakes – Llyn Alwen, Llyn Aled and Aled Isaf.* Continue ahead, soon picking up a path that skirts a reedy area to reach the top of the high pass of Bwlch y Garnedd at a prominent new viewpoint. Descend the wide embanked old green road.

6 After a few hundred yards, by a large boulder on the left, head half-LEFT down

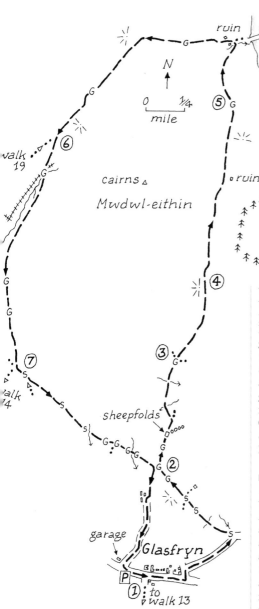

to go through a gate in the fence in the side valley below. Cross the stream and follow a path RIGHT. The path contours across reed, heather and bracken terrain, with higher ground to your left. *If there is any doubt where the path is, just watch the sheep ahead of you!* After a while, the path swings away from the side valley to go through a gate in a fence. Follow the boundary on your right through open pasture and another gate. Continue ahead, and at the wall corner, go down half-RIGHT to rejoin the Mynydd Hiraethog trail by a waymark post.

7 Follow the wall on your right, go over a stile and through a wall gap. Pass another waymark post (*the direction indicated is misleading*) and on along a grassy ridge, past another post, and on over a stile. Keep ahead alongside the wall, over a stile and a stream, and on through a gate in the field corner – *with a good view of Llyn y Cwrt.* Go through a gate ahead, and follow a track down over a river and on to the crossroad of walled tracks met at point **2**. Turn RIGHT and follow the enclosed track down to a house. Turn RIGHT through a gate at the end of the house, then swing LEFT and follow its access track to the A5 by the garage. Turn LEFT back to the start.

WALK 16

CWM MERDDWR

DESCRIPTION A 5¾ mile walk (**A**) exploring the undulating countryside of the Merddwr valley near Pentrefoelas. The route features a delightful old enclosed drovers way, a historical house, a 12thC motte and excellent views. Allow about 3 hours. A shorter 3¾ mile walk (**B**) is included.

START Car park, Pentrefoelas [SH 874 514]

DIRECTIONS From Cerrigydrudion take the A5 towards Betws-y-Coed to reach Pentrefoelas. In the village centre turn left over the river to a large car park and nearby toilets.

Pentrefoelas is an attractive estate village built by the Wynne family for its workers and craftsmen. Its water-powered mill, which still remains, was used to ground grain for bread or animal fodder. It was once an important gathering place for cattle and drovers, and in the 19thC a stopping place on Telford's London-Holyhead coach road. The 3 storey Foelas Arms Hotel was enlarged in 1839 when it took on the licence from a well known coaching house situated at Cernioge, some 2¼ miles to the east. The village now boasts an hotel, craft shop, gallery, and a post office/general stores/cafe.

It is associated with fairies and folklore. One tale involves Huw Llwyd, a famous Welsh sorcerer, who lived in Snowdonia. While staying at Pentrefoelas, he was approached by four thieves who thought he was a drover returning from the English market with money. He caused them to be transfixed overnight by a magic horn, which vanished when they were arrested the following morning!

1 Go back towards the A5, then take a waymarked path on the left by the bridge over the river Merddwr. Walk alongside the river and after about 250 yards at a stream, go half-LEFT to follow the waymarked path through a gateway. Now go half-LEFT up past a clump of trees to go through a gate in the wall. Go up the field to cross the ladder-stile ahead – *with views of the mountains of Snowdonia*. Turn LEFT and follow the

boundary round to go through a gate. Turn LEFT and drop down to go through a gate in the field corner at a waymarked path junction.

2 Turn LEFT through an adjoining gate and follow the green track – *part of the original late 18thC London-Holyhead coach road* – to a road junction. Swing RIGHT along the Ysbyty Ifan road, and after about 250 yards, cross a waymarked stile on the left. Follow a faint green track up open pasture. Cross a stile and go past a barn/caravan, and up the green track to cross a stile by a gate. Continue with the track by a stream, and at the next gateway, swing LEFT along the field edge to cross a gate in the corner. Continue along the edge of the next field to cross a ladder-stile by Plas Iolyn. Go ahead to pass the right corner of the barn, and on between outbuildings and the house to follow its access drive to a lane. *Plas Iolyn, with its 18thC wing, is dominated by the stone 'Great Barn' built high up on a rock. The house was once occupied by the notorious Dr. Ellis Price, a Doctor of Law, whose red robe earned him the name of 'Dr. Coch' (Red Doctor). His son, Capt. Thomas Price – a seafaring man and poet, along with Capt. Will Myddelton of Denbigh, are said to have been the first men to 'drink' (smoke) tobacco in public in this country.*

3 Swing sharp RIGHT along the lane. *About 50 yards after passing a small sheepfold, you catch a glimpse over the wall of the distant 17thC Giler gatehouse amongst the trees. Giler itself, dating from the 16thC was once the home of poet Rhys Wynn and the Price family descended from Cardinal Wolsey's cross-bearer.* When the lane bends left, continue on the waymarked path through a gate ahead. Now follow a delightful old enclosed gated green drovers' road that skirts Bryn Prys – *later offering superb views of the mountains of Snowdonia.* After about ¾ mile the route joins a more defined track coming from farm buildings. Continue with the enclosed track. (*For* **Walk B**, *200 yards further on, cross a stile on the right and follow the waymarked Mynydd Hiraethog path along an enclosed green*

walks 17 & 18

motte

⑤

Pentrefoelas

A5

N

0   ¼
mile

②

⑤ (P) ①

Plas
Iolyn

walk
18

walk 18

③ walk
18

Bryn Prys

④

left of a stream. Cross it near a gateway and continue up the field to go through a gate in the top corner. Walk up the field edge and at a gateway swing half-LEFT with the fence to go through a gate in the top corner. Continue alongside the wall, through two gates above a farm, and on along the edge of the next field to reach a road.

5 Go along the driveway opposite, passing Voelas Uchaf, to reach a waymarked path junction. Up to your left is the remains of Foel Las Motte – *an earth castle, which once supported a square stone tower, built about 1164.* Turn RIGHT to pass between buildings at Hen Foelas – *site of the original main home of the Wynnes from 1545-1819* – to drop down through the trees. Go straight across the large field and through a small gate in the wall corner. Go down the edge of the next field, through another gate, then swing half-LEFT

to pass between houses to the road. Turn LEFT and follow the road to reach the A5 by the Foelas Arms Hotel, *where refreshments are available.* Cross the road back to the start.

track down to pass through a farm and along its access track to the road. Turn right, then left along a track to rejoin your outward route.)

4 At a road turn RIGHT and follow it for about ⅓ mile. About 80 yards after passing the entrance to Gwernhywel-ganol, drop down LEFT off the road to cross a gate onto an old reedy enclosed green track. Follow it, soon dropping gently down the hillside to meet a lane/track junction. Continue down the lane to reach the A5 opposite a house. Cross the road and go through a wooden gate by a waymark post. Head up the field to the

Foelas Arms Hotel

WALK 17
FOEL LAS MOTTE & FFRIDD-Y-FOEL

DESCRIPTION A 5-mile figure of eight walk through the varied countryside of the Voelas estate. The route passes an old earthwork castle, before following a lane and green track up to the edge of moorland, reaching a height of just over 1100 feet. It then follows an old drovers road around the slopes of Ffridd-y-foel, passing an unexpected example of estate enterprise, before returning on a choice of routes. Allow about 3 hours. The route can easily be shortened to a 2-mile walk, or extended on a good track across moorland to the remote Llyn Alwen, adding 4 miles to the distance. (See **Walk 19** map)
START Car park, Pentrefoelas [SH 874 514]
See **Walk 16**.

1 Cross the A5 by the Foelas Arms Hotel, and walk through the village, soon swinging LEFT with the road over the river. Go past an old cast iron water pump, and just beyond the old school, turn RIGHT on a path signposted 'Foel Las Motte' passing between houses to enter a field. Go half-LEFT and through a small gate in the corner. Continue up the field edge, through another small gate, then follow a green track across the next field to go through a gate into the wood ahead. Follow a stony track rising through the trees, then pass between buildings at Hen Voelas to reach a waymarked path junction by an access track. *Only a small altered cottage remains of the original cluster of buildings of Hen Voelas (Old Voelas) – the original main home of the Wynnes from 1545-1819. Voelas Hall, just over a mile to the west, became the estate home.* Continue ahead on the waymarked Mynydd Hiraethog trail through the wood. *Up to your right is the tree-topped mound of Foel Las Motte. Reputedly made by Owain Gwynedd about 1164, this tall earth castle once supported a square stone tower. Its use ceased in 1185. On your left is a large rectangular pool, which provided water for Pentrefoelas Mill.* Go through a gate and on along the field edge to reach a lane.

2 Turn RIGHT. (*For the **shorter** walk turn left to point **7**.*) Go past a track/footpath sign (*your return route*) and keep with the lane as it rises steadily up the hillside. After about ½ mile, just after passing over a cattle-grid, turn LEFT by a waymark post to follow a track past the edge of a wood and up to go through a gate into open upland country. *Pause to enjoy the extensive views of Snowdonia.* Continue with the track, passing through two further gates, to reach a way-marked path junction. (*Here you can follow the track ahead for 2 miles across moorland to the remote lake of Llyn Alwen. It is a there and back option, but the track and views are enjoyable both ways.*)

3 Leave the Mynydd Hiraethog trail by turning LEFT. Walk through a reedy area to the right of an old boundary and stream to follow the line of an old green track – *the remains of a drovers road. It bears away from the boundary to ford a stream by a wall/fence. Upstream is a small waterfall.* Continue ahead, soon alongside a substantial wall. *To your right is a vast area of wild remote moorland.* Go through a gate in the wall corner and an enclosed gated sheepfold, and on along a wall-enclosed section of track. *The high wall on your right is a superb example of dry stone walling. One can only marvel at the skill, patience and time consuming effort that went into its construction in such a wild and inhospitable environment, exposed to the elements. The wall is superior in quality to others nearby. But why? A door mid-way deepens the mystery. A farmer later told me that it is a large walled enclosure known as 'The Warren'. It was built for hare-breeding by Voelas estate, presumably at a time when jugged, roast, boiled, potted and hashed hare were culinary delights!*

4 After going through a gate continue with the old track alongside the wall. *Cattle still graze the upland pastures – a reminder of times gone by when animals were fattened on these slopes before being taken by drovers to distant markets.* Follow the track

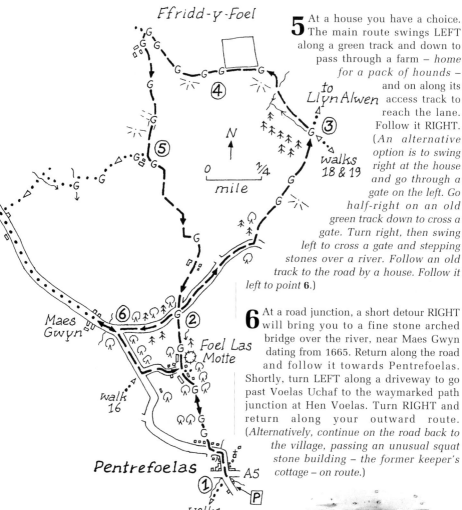

Ffridd-y-Foel

N

to
Llyn Alwen

walks
18 & 19

0   ¼
mile

④

⑤

③

②

⑥

Maes
Gwyn

Foel Las
Motte

walk
16

Pentrefoelas   A5

①   **P**

walks
16 & 18

5 At a house you have a choice. The main route swings LEFT along a green track and down to pass through a farm – *home for a pack of hounds* – and on along its access track to reach the lane. Follow it RIGHT. (*An alternative option is to swing right at the house and go through a gate on the left. Go half-right on an old green track down to cross a gate. Turn right, then swing left to cross a gate and stepping stones over a river. Follow an old track to the road by a house. Follow it left to point* **6**.)

6 At a road junction, a short detour RIGHT will bring you to a fine stone arched bridge over the river, near Maes Gwyn dating from 1665. Return along the road and follow it towards Pentrefoelas. Shortly, turn LEFT along a driveway to go past Voelas Uchaf to the waymarked path junction at Hen Voelas. Turn RIGHT and return along your outward route. (*Alternatively, continue on the road back to the village, passing an unusual squat stone building – the former keeper's cottage – on route.*)

Water pump

through two further gates, then turn LEFT down a gated enclosed track towards a farm. After going through a gate at the bottom, immediately turn LEFT over another gate. Go alongside the boundary, through a gap in the wall, and on with the wall on your left to pass through an open gateway ahead in the corner. Go half-RIGHT across the next field to cross a gate near the corner. Keep ahead to the far wall boundary, then follow it RIGHT to go through a gate and continue along a track.

WALK 18
THE PENTREFOELAS ROUND

DESCRIPTION A 7½-mile walk (**A**) or shorter 4½ mile walk (**B**), using paths, old coaching and drovers routes and quiet lanes, through open countryside around Pentrefoelas, with excellent views throughout. The route rises in stages to Bryn Prys at just over 1000 feet before descending to pass by an historical house and on to the hamlet of Rhydlydan, with its country inn. It then meanders north to skirt moorland, reaching over 1100 feet, before descending to Pentrefoelas. Allow about 4 hours.
START Car park, Pentrefoelas [SH 874 514] See **Walk 16**.

1 Follow instructions in the first section of **Walk 16**.

2 Turn RIGHT along a green track – *part of the original late 18thC London-Holyhead coach road.* At a track junction, follow the track LEFT to a road. Turn RIGHT and after 100 yards, go LEFT up a stony track to follow a waymarked path through Gallt-y-celyn farm. Continue up a green track, soon becoming enclosed to cross a stile onto a stony track. Turn LEFT along the track and, when it bends right, continue ahead on a green track – *an old drovers route.*

3 About 100 yards after going through a gate, cross a waymarked stile on the left and a wall, then go half-RIGHT up the gorse covered slopes of Bryn Prys, soon crossing the bend of a green track. Continue past the end of a small plantation and on across a reedy area to go through a hidden gate in the wall ahead. Go onto the small ridge to enjoy the panoramic views. Drop down the slope towards Plas Iolyn, passing to the left of a rock escarpment, to join a green track by a plantation. Follow it to pass through a second gate by the corner of another small plantation. Go ahead towards the stone 'Great

Barn'of Plas Iolyn, turn LEFT through another gate, then bear RIGHT to pass between outbuildings and the house and along its driveway to a lane. (*See* **Walk 15** *for information on Plas Iolyn.*) Follow the lane ahead – *a continuation of the earlier drovers route* – over a crossroad – *the line of a Roman road from Bala to Conwy* – and on to reach a road junction at Rhydlydan. Turn LEFT to the Giler Arms Hotel, where refreshments are available. *Nearby, in 1820, during construction of Telford's new road (the A5) 40 longcist graves were uncovered and a 5th–6thC inscribed stone found. It commemorated Brohomaglus Iattus and his wife Caune, and indicated links with Christians in southern Gaul.*

4 Continue along the road – *a section of the old London–Holyhead coach road that Telford's road replaced* – to drop down to a junction by a 19thC chapel. Here, turn RIGHT by a waymark post to go along the access track to Pentre Felin. Pass in front of the house to go through a gate. Immediately turn RIGHT to pass to the left of stone outbuildings, then drop down to cross a footbridge over the river and on up to the A5. Cross the road WITH CARE and the stile opposite. Go up the edge of a reedy field, through a field gap, and then a gate into the old farmyard of Cefngarw. (*For* **Walk B** *go left and follow an enclosed green track to the A543. Cross the road and follow it left, then turn right on a waymarked path. Go between a cluster of buildings and on across fields to Pentrefoelas.*)

5 For the main route turn RIGHT and follow an old green track for ⅓ mile to cross a gate by a cottage. Follow its access track to the bend of a lane. Continue ahead, and at a road junction, turn LEFT and follow the lane past a cottage to cross a delightful stone slab bridge over a river. At the next junction, follow the lane LEFT to reach the A543. Turn RIGHT along the road, then turn LEFT up a lane past a telephone box and a cottage. When it bends towards a farm, continue up a waymarked enclosed green track. After going through a gate, swing RIGHT up a wider enclosed track. *Like the one just left, this is*

an old drovers route used to move
animals to markets in Denbigh
and further afield in Cheshire
and Shropshire. After going
through a set of gates at its end,
continue with the line of the old
green track alongside the
boundary as it contours the
slopes of Cefnen Wen, passing through further gates.
Eventually it descends
gently to a crossroad
of tracks by a way-
mark post.

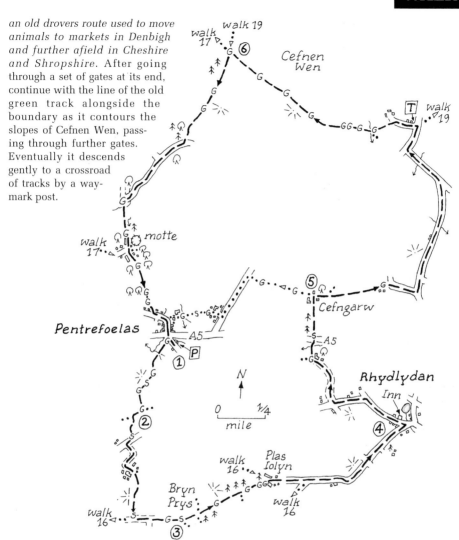

6 Turn LEFT through a gate and follow a
delightful green track – *with superb views
ahead* – to drop down to a lane. Follow it
RIGHT to steadily descend. Just before a cattle grid, turn LEFT through a kissing gate by
a waymark post. Walk along the field edge
and through a wood past a small reservoir.
*Up to your left is the remains of Foel Las
Motte – an earth castle, which once supported a square stone tower, built about 1164.* At
a waymark post and track continue ahead to

pass between buildings at Hen Foelas – *site
of the original main home of the Wynnes
from 1545-1819* – and drop down through
the trees. Go on across a large field to go
through a small gate in the wall corner. Go
down the field edge, through another gate,
then swing half-LEFT to pass between houses to the road. Turn LEFT and follow the
road through the village to the A5 by the
Foelas Arms Hotel, where refreshments are
available.

WALK 19

THE THREE LAKES TRAIL

DESCRIPTION An exhilarating 10½-mile moorland walk in the heart of Mynydd Hiraethog, visiting three upland lakes of different character – Llyn Aled, the remote natural lake of Llyn Alwen, and the Alwen reservoir. *This route requires careful navigation at times and is for the experienced and well equipped walker who likes wild open moorland.* It is best undertaken on a clear sunny day, when the treeless landscape is magical and the panoramic views superb. The initial section to Llyn Alwen is the most demanding, crossing largely pathless and sometimes boggy moorland. It is then followed by a superb 2-mile green track across remote moorland, and then an old drovers' route. The return follows the route of a medieval road up Bwlch y Garnedd and down to cross the Alwen reservoir for an easy final section along bridleways and road. Allow about 5½ - 6 hours.

START The dam, Llyn Aled. [SH 916579]

DIRECTIONS From the A543 Denbigh-Pentrefoelas road take the minor road signposted to Llyn Aled to park by the lake just before it crosses the dam.

1 Follow instructions in the first section of Walk 20.

2 Drop down through a reedy area and on up to the inauspicious top of Moel Llyn ahead. Now go half-LEFT down towards the tops of two trees near the right hand end of Llyn Alwen, soon picking up a steadily improving path. When it splits take the RIGHT fork, then swing RIGHT around a depression and on past a red-topped post. Drop down via a gate to the old farm of Ty'n-llyn below. *This idyllic location beside the hidden beauty of this remote lake, surrounded by wild and inhospitable moorland makes a gem of a stop on a fine day – a haven of peace and tranquility.* Leave the farm by its green access track alongside the lake edge. After going through a gate you quickly leave

the lake behind to follow the delightful green track for 2 miles across the expansive wild moorland. *After the earlier rough crossing it is a pleasure to stride out on this safe passage through such a wild landscape, enjoying the superb views. After going through a second gate there are good views of Moel Hebog, the Nantlle ridge, Snowdon, the Glyders, Tryfan and the Carneddau.* Eventually the track reaches a waymark post at a track junction just before a gate.

3 Turn LEFT on the waymarked Mynydd Hiraethog trail and follow an old gated green track – variable in quality – alongside a wall, contouring the mid-slopes of Cefnen Wen. *This is an old drovers route used to move animals to markets in Denbigh and further afield in Cheshire and Shropshire.* After a double set of gates, the track becomes enclosed and begins to descend. About 150 yards after passing through another gate, at the broadest section of the track, swing LEFT through a waymarked gate. Now follow another enclosed track to drop down past a farm, and continue down its access lane to the A543. Go through the waymarked gate opposite, then go half-LEFT to cross a footbridge over a stream. Continue up the slope ahead to follow a wide enclosed track past farm buildings to go through a second gate into open country.

4 Continue ahead alongside the old wall to join and follow an enclosed track, soon swinging half-LEFT. After going through a gate, keep with this delightful, but steadily deteriorating track, as it rises gently across open upland pasture. Go through a gate just above the track and continue ahead to pass by a small ruin. Continue along the line of the old track. *Note the many lichen-covered stones.* At a more distinct crosstrack, turn RIGHT and soon follow the line of the old embanked Pentrefoelas-Denbigh road rising up Bwlch y Garnedd. *This ancient road fell out of use after the building of the turnpike road, now the A543, in 1826.* After passing a large squat stone, continue with a clear path along the right side of the old road to reach the top of the bwlch. *Up to the right is the cairned top of heather covered Mwdwl-*

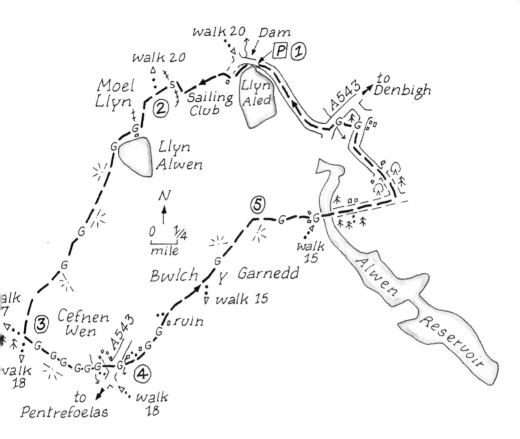

eithin. A boulder near the top of the pass makes a good place for a break to enjoy the views, soon to disappear. From the top of the bwlch can be seen Llyn Aled and Llyn Alwen. Pass to the right of a reedy area, then go half-LEFT to continue with the line of the road, now a faint track, to go through a gate in the fence ahead. Continue with the faint reed-covered track heading north-east along the wide ridge.

5 At its end, with a good view of Alwen reservoir, go half-RIGHT with the track, for a while more distinct, to drop down through a gate to reach the sparse remains of a former upland farm – *enjoying panoramic views of Alwen reservoir on route.* From the solitary tree, swing half-RIGHT past sheep-

folds to a waymark post. Continue ahead in the direction of Pen-y-ffrith to cross a long footbridge over the neck of the reservoir. Continue up a stony track (a bridleway) past the house of Pen-y-ffrith, and keep with the track for about ½ mile. At a waymarked bridleway junction, turn LEFT to follow another track, soon descending past the entrance to Hafod Elwy Hall and the large stone outbuilding of Tan-y-graig farm. Continue with the access track, then at the next farm, turn LEFT through a gate opposite a barn. Go past a small plantation and follow the fence round to cross a gate above a stream to reach the A543. Cross the road and follow it LEFT. Shortly turn RIGHT along the road back to Llyn Aled. *The expansive beauty of the lake makes an enjoyable finale to the walk.*

WALK 20

AROUND ALED ISAF

DESCRIPTION This 8-mile walk explores the expansive tract of moorland and upland pasture in the northern part of Mynydd Hiraethog near the upland lakes of Llyn Aled and Isaf Aled, offering extensive views, with a wet start and a dry finish! The route crosses moorland just west of Llyn Aled, before heading north across a moorland plateau. The main route (**A**) follows a delightful upland track, with an alternative parallel route (**B**) continuing through moorland/pastureland. Both routes return across a moorland top, then follow an attractive upland road, passing by a dramatic gorge and Rhaeadr y Bedd waterfall, and on alongside Aled Isaf. *This route is for the experienced walker, for its outward route crosses wild moorland – boggy in parts – and requires careful navigation.* **It should be avoided in poor visibility.** Allow about 4½ hours.
START The dam, Llyn Aled [SH 916579]
DIRECTIONS From the A543 Denbigh-Pentrefoelas road take the minor road signposted to Llyn Aled to park by the lake just before it crosses the dam.

1 From the castellated stone building that controls the outflow from Llyn Aled, built in 1934 as a regulating reservoir, walk along the edge of the lake towards the sailing club, crossing a stream and a fence. At the slipway swing RIGHT to cross a stile by the access gate/track. Go up a green track ahead. It soon swings LEFT and ends after about 100 yards. Continue straight ahead, and after a few yards, take the right fork of a path. It heads west across moorland along the left hand edge of a shallow valley, passing on the higher ground to your right, a descending tree/hedge boundary and then a small stone sheepfold. At the slight head of the valley, leave the path, which bends left, and continue straight ahead. Work your way across the right hand side of an expanse of boggy moorland to reach a fence near its corner, where stands an old inscribed slate boundary stone.

Turn RIGHT and walk alongside the fence, rising gently to cross an old stile in the fence on a small ridge, after a few hundred yards. Now go up onto the top of the ridge to enjoy the extensive views – *south east over Llyn Aled to Clocaenog Forest; south to Alwen reservoir and the distant Berwyns; south west a glimpse of Llyn Alwen and the distant Arans, Arenig and Rhinogs; to the north west the Carneddau range and Tryfan. To the east, prominent on the skyline is the ruin of Gwylfa Hiraethog – the former shooting lodge of Viscount Devonport (details in* **Walk 7**). Walk along its broad top.

2 After about 200 yards swing sharp RIGHT across the moorland plateau – to cross an old gate in the fence, about 150 yards beyond another boundary stone. Continue straight ahead northwards, by a reedy area, across the wide expanse of moorland, aiming for the eastern end of a distant green ridge. After a few hundred yards, you will pick up a clear path, with drier conditions underfoot. Soon the path parallels a fence on your left. After crossing a stream near the fence, go up the slope ahead and past sheepfolds. Follow the fence down to a gate in the corner.

3 Here you have a choice. *(For route* **B**, *head half-right, at first near the fence and stream, towards distant small plantations, down to cross an old gate. Follow an old boundary embankment ahead and cross a gate at its end. Keep alongside the fenced embankment on your right. At its corner, continue up the slope ahead and across the small flat hilltop of Bryn Poeth. As you begin a gentle descent, cross a stile in the fence on your left. Go half-right, through a gate and on across the middle of a green field, leaving it by a gate. Keep ahead down the field by a small gorge to reach a lane at point* **5**.) For route **A**, go through the gate and another one nearby. Go over a stream and follow a rising green track up through a gate onto the grassy ridge of Llys Dymper. At a track junction, swing RIGHT, pass through a gate, and follow this delightful level upland track – *enjoying the excellent views; west to the mountains of Snowdonia; north east to the Clwydian Hills.*

4 After about 1 mile, the track begins to descend, then levels out. After passing a derelict cottage it becomes a lane. Follow it down to meet two waymark posts at a cross path. Here turn RIGHT and cross the fence into a field. Go ahead, soon descending to go through a gate below a derelict cottage. Turn LEFT, through another gate, then go half-RIGHT along a green track. Keep with the LEFT fork to cross a gate. Follow the gently rising track across the reedy terrain alongside a stream, swinging LEFT through a gate. Keep on alongside the stream, over another, and on along the field edge, past sheepfolds. At the fence corner, turn LEFT to reach the bend of a lane.

5 Follow the lane RIGHT and just past Tyny-ffynnon, cross the fence on the right by an old metal sign. Now head half-LEFT to reach the boundary fence by Tan-y-foel, then follow the boundary RIGHT up to cross a gate in the field corner. Keep straight ahead, soon on a faint green track to cross the wide moorland top of Foel Lwyd and then drop down alongside a fence. At its corner, swing LEFT through a reedy area to reach the road by a ruined cottage. Turn RIGHT along the road, soon descending to cross the dam of Aled Isaf – a regulating reservoir built in the 1930s – by an impressive gorge containing Rhaeadr y Bedd waterfall. During 1974, low water levels revealed flint artefacts and other evidence on the reservoir bed of occupation by mesolithic hunter/gatherers, who roamed through this area when a gentler climate and woodland habitat made it a less hostile environment. Continue with the road alongside the lake and on back to Llyn Aled.

Boundary stone

Map labels

Tynyffynnon
Foel Lwyd
Bryn Poeth
Route A
Route B
Llys Dymper
sheepfold
Aled Isaf
Afon Aled
Rhaeadr y Bedd
N
0   ¼ mile
Dam
P
boundary stone
Sailing Club
Llyn Aled
boundary stone
walk 19
walk 19

WALK 21
AROUND CWM CLEDWEN

DESCRIPTION A 6-mile walk (**A**) exploring the hills on both sides of the Cledwen valley in which lies the remote ancient community of Gwytherin on the northern edges of Mynydd Hiraethog. It offers extensive views, especially of the mountains of Snowdonia. The route rises steadily to reach upland pasture at over 1200 feet, before descending back into Cwm Cledwen. It then rises up an attractive side valley and across an expansive moorland plateau, reaching a height of over 1300 feet, before descending to Gwytherin. Allow about 4 hours. By utilising the quiet valley road, the route can easily be undertaken as two separate walks of 4 (**B**) and 4½ (**C**) miles.

START Gwytherin [SH 876615]

DIRECTIONS Gwytherin lies 4 miles south west of Llansannan on the B5384. Park tidily in the village.

Gwytherin is a remote community, with an important ecclesiastical past. The church, dedicated to St. Winifred, was built in 1869 to replace an earlier one. Legend has it that St. Winifred, associated with the 'holy well' in Holywell, later came to Gwytherin, where she became abbess at a local nunnery in the 12thC. After her death her remains were kept in the former church, but were eventually transferred to Shrewsbury. The churchyard contains old yew trees, and on the north side of the church stand a line of 4 small standing stones. One, dating from the 5th-6thC and inscribed in Latin, commemorates Vinne-maglus. Such stones provided the earliest evidence of Christianity. In the village centre on the site of a former smithy is a plaque to one of its famous sons, Clwydfardd (1800–94), the first Archdruid.

1 Leave the village centre along the road signposted to Denbigh/Llansannan. (*Or, for* **Walk C**, *the road south to point* **3**) After about 20 yards, turn RIGHT along a 'No through road'. Follow the lane past the community centre, over the Afon Cledwen and on through a cluster of farm buildings. When the lane ends at another farm bear LEFT past a stone outbuilding, through a gate and on up a concrete track. It soon becomes stony as it rises steadily up the eastern slopes of the Cledwen valley. Just after going through a gate where the track levels out and splits – *with excellent views west across the valley to the mountain peaks of Snowdonia* – swing LEFT through a gate to follow the rising stony track.

2 After a few hundred yards, when the track begins to bear half-left, go through a gate immediately ahead. Continue across enclosed upland pasture and through a gate in the boundary ahead. Keep ahead to pass through a gate in the embanked fence boundary. Now go half-RIGHT down the edge of a gully/stream to the end of a ruined upland dwelling. Cross the stream and fence, then go half-LEFT and through a gate by a track. Follow the track past sheepfolds – *enjoying extensive open views south into the heart of Mynydd Hiraethog*. Soon it swings left and goes through a gate. Ignore the track swinging right. Instead go half-RIGHT to join a short section of old sunken green track down open pasture. At a cross-track bear half-RIGHT to cross an old gate in the boundary. Walk ahead parallel with the fence on your right towards the panorama of mountains. *On a clear day, dominating the skyline, from left to right, are Moel Siabod, Snowdon, the Glyders, Tryfan, and the Carnaddau range.* After about 200 yards, head half-LEFT to join a faint green track beneath a small grassy knoll to go through a gate in the fence. Continue ahead to drop down the hillside to go through a gate in the fence corner above a deep side valley. Now follow a green track down alongside the boundary embankment. It then swings sharp LEFT down to ford a stream. Continue past a farm and on to cross a footbridge over the river onto a road. Follow the road RIGHT.

3 Turn LEFT up the access track to Tai Pellaf. (*Or for* **Walk B** *follow the road back along the valley*). After passing a large barn, swing RIGHT and go through a gate by a stream. Follow a track up the attractive side valley. When it splits, with one branch swinging sharp right, keep ahead to cross a conflu-ence of streams, then swing RIGHT with the track up the left hand side of the valley. After going through a gate, fol-low the track up the reedy moorland to reach a lane. Follow it RIGHT, and after about 300 yards go through a way-marked gate on your left (*or alternatively follow the lane down to Gwytherin*). Go on across upland pasture and through the lower of two gates in the fence ahead. Now go half-LEFT to cross a way-marked stile in a fence corner, and on across moorland near the fence on your left – *enjoy-ing good views of the Snowdonia mountains and the Conwy valley.* Go through a gate in the fence corner and continue by the fence.

4 Go past a waymarked stile and on with the fence along the moorland/upland edge to reach a wide track. Follow it RIGHT, steadily descending to cross a stream. Keep with the main track and just before an old cottage, cross a waymarked stile on the right to pass behind the building and on over a stile. Go ahead to descend the upland pasture to the left of a narrow wooded side valley. Soon, you pass a large area of gorse to reach the end of an old embanked field boundary. Drop down through the trees with the boundary on your left. Follow an improving path descending the edge of the wooded valley moving steadily closer to the

stream below. Cross a stile and follow the stream down past a house and on to reach the road by the Red Lion.

View towards the mountains of Snowdonia

PRONUNCIATION

These basic points should help non-Welsh speakers

Welsh	English equivalent
c	always hard, as in **c**at
ch	as in the Scottish word lo**ch**
dd	as th in **th**en
f	as v in **v**ocal
ff	as **f**
g	always hard as in **g**ot
ll	no real equivalent. It is like 'th' in **th**en, but with an 'L' sound added to it, giving '**thlan**' for the pronunciation of the Welsh 'Llan'.

In Welsh the accent usually falls on the last-but-one syllable of a word.

KEY TO THE MAPS

- **—▶** Walk route and direction
- **═══** Metalled road
- **‑ ‑ ‑** Unsurfaced road
- **• • • •** Footpath/route adjoining walk route
- **~~~** River/stream
- **⋆ ۿ** Trees
- **■▄■** Railway
- **G** Gate
- **S** Stile
- **F.B.** Footbridge
- **⩘** Viewpoint
- **Ⓟ** Parking
- **Ⓣ** Telephone
- **🚐** Caravan site

THE COUNTRY CODE

Enjoy the countryside and respect its life and work

Guard against all risk of fire

Leave gates *as you find them*

Keep your dogs under close control

Keep to public paths across farmland

Use gates and stiles to cross fences, hedges and walls

Leave livestock, crops and machinery alone

Take your litter home

Help to keep all water clean

Protect wildlife, plants and trees

Take special care on country roads

Make no unnecessary noise

I wish to thank Piers Warburton, former ranger at the Llyn Brenig Centre, and his colleagues; Denbighshire Countryside Service; and Conwy County Borough Council Highways Department for responding to referred footpath problems in their areas.
David Berry

Published by
Kittiwake
3 Glantwymyn Village Workshops,
Cemmaes Road, Machynlleth, Montgomeryshire
SY20 8LY

© Text & map research: David Berry 2001
© Maps & illustrations: Kittiwake 2001
Illustrations by Morag Perrott
Cover photographs: David Berry – large: Llyn Alwen (Walk **19**); inset: Bagot's Monument, Pincyn Llys (Walks **3** & **4**).

Printed by WPG, Welshpool, Powys

ISBN: 1 902302 15 X